Cognitive Behavioural Therapy

The Key Lessons for Beginners on How CBT is used in Retraining the Brain to Overcome Depression, Anxiety and Negative Thinking Using Practical Techniques and Hypnosis

Tom Wallaces   Daniel Shepherd

© **Copyright 2018 by Tom Wallaces & Daniel Shepherd - All rights reserved.**

The content contained within this book may not be reproduced, duplicated or transmitted without direct written permission from the author or the publisher.

Under no circumstances will any blame or legal responsibility be held against the publisher, or author, for any damages, reparation, or monetary loss due to the information contained within this book. Either directly or indirectly.

Legal Notice:

This book is copyright protected. This book is only for personal use. You cannot amend, distribute, sell, use, quote or paraphrase any part, or the content within this book, without the consent of the author or publisher.

Disclaimer Notice:

Please note the information contained within this document is for educational and entertainment purposes only. All effort has been executed to present accurate, up to date, and reliable, complete information. No warranties of any kind are declared or implied. Readers acknowledge that the author is not engaging in the rendering of legal, financial, medical or professional advice. The content within this book has been derived from various sources. Please consult a licensed professional before attempting any techniques outlined in this book.

By reading this document, the reader agrees that under no circumstances is the author responsible for any losses, direct or indirect, which are incurred as a result of the use of information contained within this document, including, but not limited to, — errors, omissions, or inaccuracies.

Contents

Introduction 1

Your Thought Process 5

    Types of thinking 6

        Perceptual thinking 6

        Conceptual thinking 6

        Reflective thinking 7

        Creative thinking 7

        Critical thinking 8

        Non-directed thinking 9

    Development of Thinking 10

    Thinking tools 13

    Automatic Intrusive Thoughts 16

    The Voices in your Head 21

    How changing your thought process can change your life 27

What is Cognitive Behavioral Therapy? 31

Cognitive therapy 34

Behavior therapy 34

How to go about getting CBT? 35

History of CBT 38

Types of CBT 40

   Brief cognitive behavioral therapy or BCBT ... 41

   Cognitive-emotional behavioral therapy or CEBT 42

   Structure cognitive behavioral training or SCBT 42

   Moral reconation therapy 43

   Stress inoculation training 43

   Mindfulness-based cognitive behavioral therapy 45

   Unified protocol 45

   Pros and Cons of CBT 46

   Differences between CBT and other psychotherapies: 48

Cognitive Distortion 49

Awareness 49

What are cognitive disorders? 49

Symptoms of cognitive disorders 51

Effects of cognitive disorders 52

    Treatment 53

Common cognitive distortions 55

Cognitive Restructuring 61

Depression & Anxiety 65

Depression 65

Symptoms of depression 68

Types of depression 68

Causes of depression 71

Treatments for depression 72

Anxiety 74

Causes of anxiety: 76

Journaling 78

Tips for journaling: 82

Does journaling help to treat depression? 85

Gratitude 87

Benefits of journaling: 88

Precautions while journaling: 90

Mindfulness Meditation 92

Mindfulness-integrated Cognitive Behavior Therapy 95

Dealing with Negative Thinking and Self-Talk 100

Types of negative thinking: 102

Effect of negative thinking: 104

Changing your belief system 105

How to stop negative thoughts and negative self-talk 107

Reducing Stress 110

Symptoms of stress: 112

Benefits of CBT for stress: 113

How to make your life less stressful? 116

Hypnotherapy 120

Misconceptions about Hypnotherapy: 124

Focusing on the Future 127

Getting Rid of Toxic Connections 127

How to let go of the past and build the new you? 138

How to stay positive every day? 145

Quick Fix Tips to stay Positive 147

Relapse 154

Precautions **155**

Conclusion **158**

Introduction

I want to thank you for choosing this book, 'Cognitive Behavioral Therapy: The Key Lessons for Beginners on How CBT is used in Retraining the Brain to Overcome Depression, Anxiety and Negative Thinking Using Practical Techniques and Hypnosis' and hope that it helps you understand Cognitive Behavioral Therapy or CBT as it is commonly called.

You probably go in for a regular health check-up every six months or at least once a year. Every time you fall sick or hurt yourself, you probably consult a doctor. But these are all physical injuries and most people only pay heed to these. Somehow, being able to see a cut or bruise makes it a valid illness, but something we can't see or understand is ignored.

At some point or the other, everyone has negative feelings, depression, or stress. Did you ever consult someone to deal with it? Usually, people just like to work through it by them and are somehow ashamed of admitting they need help. You need to understand that physical injuries need care, but a little medicine and some bandages will heal them up quickly. Mental health, however, is just as important but more complicated to deal with. Feeling sad about something for a while is completely different from suffering from depression, mental trauma, and just illnesses. There is never any shame in admitting that your mind needs some healing and that you need to reach out for help.

Mental issues can be much more complex than you realize and need professional help. Over the past couple of years, mental health has been gaining a lot more attention as people realize that it is just as crucial as physical health. When was the last time you looked for treatment for mental issues that are affecting your daily life and mental stability? You do not have to compare your problems with others and feel like yours are not big enough to deserve attention. Everyone has his or her own issues, and each one is equally valid and deserves to be addressed.

One of the treatments that are used for dealing with mental health issues like depression, personality disorders, stress, etc. is Cognitive Behavioral Therapy. This book will help you understand what this therapy is and how it can help in mental health treatment. If you are reading this book, you have taken the first step to admitting that you need help. Learning about Cognitive Behavioral Therapy will help you understand the methods involved in it and will help you utilize it to restore peace to your mind. This therapy has involved a lot of study and research and is used to treat anxiety, depression, addictions, stress, and such issues that can seriously affect your mental health and daily life.

Mental illness is just as common and important as physical illness. If you leave it untreated for too long, it can build up and seriously affect your daily life. Physical illness just affects your body, and at most it will leave a scar once you treat it. Mental illness will affect you and the people around you. Leaving such issues unaddressed will have a negative impact on yourself and your relationships with other people as well as your work life. All the information in this book is meant to help you in improving the quality of your thoughts and your quality of life. There are many reasons why people get stuck in bad situations, and negative thoughts are one of the main reasons for this.

Changing your mindset and dealing with mental issues will help you to turn things around for the better. You have to recognize negative behavior and thoughts and change them to achieve better things in your life. So, take a step and start the journey to gain peace in your life again.

Thank you once again for choosing this book. I hope you find it informative. the only thing I ask is if you could please leave an honest review after listening.

Chapter 1

Your Thought Process

Your thought process is how your mind works or thinks about something. Everyone has a unique mind and thus a unique way of thinking and processing things. The brain is one organ on which there is always extensive research being conducted, and yet there is never any definitive understanding of it. Each individual has a thought process by which they use their mind to carefully consider something.

Thinking and reasoning are cognitive abilities that distinguish humans from other species. Everything a person faces in life is dealt with using reasoning and their thinking capacity. The power of this process is an essential tool in survival. Thinking and reasoning are essential for everyone to lead a good life.

Types of thinking

If you want to classify thinking into types, they would be as follows:

Perceptual thinking

Perceptual thinking is the simpler form of thinking and is based on a person's perception. This means that it is how a person interprets sensations from a particular experience. This type of thinking is called concrete thinking because it is based on the perception of concrete things.

Conceptual thinking

Also known as abstract thinking, conceptual thinking allows a person to make use of generalized concepts. It is considered superior to concrete thinking because it involves some effort in solving problems and understanding things.

Reflective thinking

Reflective thinking is the type that tries to solve complex problems. This is done by reorganizing relevant experiences concerning a situation and also by removing obstacles. The mental activity in reflective thinking does not involve trial and error efforts, so it is a more insightful approach. Reflective thinking involves rearrangement of relevant facts to reach a logical conclusion and find a solution.

Creative thinking

Creative thinking is linked with the person's ability to create a novel or new thing. It describes and interprets the nature of modern relationships. The person uses evidence and tools to find a solution. Creative thinking comes in all shapes and forms and is an entirely internal process. It is an integral part of cognitive behavior. Every person is capable of creative thinking. This type of thinking allows something new to be formed every time. Unlike convergent thinking, creative thinking involves different dimensions of thought. It covers many aspects of an individual's life and is very comprehensive.

Critical thinking

Critical thinking helps a person to step aside from their prejudices, personal beliefs or opinions and assess the truth. It is done even at the expense of disregarding a person's own belief system. This type of thinking involves higher cognitive ability and skill, and this helps in interpreting, analyzing and evaluating a situation. It helps the person to reach an inference from the unbiased gathered judgment. Critical thinking can be a self-regulatory mechanism that can be beneficial to the person. The person must have an open mind and be fair in his judgment. He cannot use bias and personal prejudices to decide on something. Their skills of interpretation, analysis, evaluation, etc. all have to be up to the mark. Critical thinking is a more complex and higher way of thinking. It utilizes cognitive skills to reach a reliable and valid judgment from the gathered information.

Non-directed thinking

Sometimes your thinking can go off in an undirected way and has no goal. It can be a unique type of thought process that is reflected in the form of dreams and random activities. This type of thinking is also said to be associative. All the dreams and delusion can be a part of withdrawal behavior where the individual tries to escape from their reality. Instead of facing the demands of their reality, they escape in fantasies which leave them non-directed and unconnected to what is around them.

Daydreaming is considered a very normal type of behavior, but when a person indulges in too many and becomes delusional, it is definitely a problem. Delusional behavior is an abnormality that strays from normal thought processes. Such delusions can make a person think they are in another role different from their reality. A man with financial issues can be deluded into thinking he is a millionaire. Someone who works a normal clerk job can think of himself as a great artist. These delusions can take any form and allow the person to escape from the reality of their situation. Sometimes these delusions can have such a grip on the mental state of the person that a perfectly healthy person thinks of himself as suffering from a chronic disease and experiences the symptoms in his mind.

Development of Thinking

A person's ability to learn things and to solve problems is dependent on their ability to think clearly. This will help them in adjusting to the demands of life and live successfully. The thought process of a person plays a definitive role in his development. If a person wants to be able to contribute something to society, his thinking has to be careful, distinct and constructive. Only then can he be capable of worthwhile contribution. People have to develop their thinking process by acquiring more knowledge and practicing a proper process of thinking. There are certain methods that help in this development process.

1. Sufficient knowledge and experience play a big role in systematic thinking. This is

important to consider while raising children; they need to be provided with an adequate amount of these to help them. Children have to be trained so that they can be more perceptive and sensitive to all thoughts and experiences. This will help to develop their process of critical thinking as well. Every individual has to be provided with sufficient opportunities to experience more. They need to practice self-study and participate in activities that are stimulating.

2. Motivation is important to mobilize thinking energy. Motivation generates genuine interest and attention in the thinking process. This helps in improving efficiency while thinking and increases adequacy as well. It is important to think in definite lines and aim for a definite purpose. Every problem we think about should be connected to immediate needs or motives.

3. There has to be enough freedom and flexibility for thinking. Unnecessary obstructions or restrictions will restrict the thought process. If what you already know

does not help you to solve a problem, think of new ways. Narrowing your field of thought can be limiting for the development of your thinking.

4. Another method that is useful while facing hard problems is incubation. Sometimes it is hard to find a solution no matter how much you think about it. At this time, you should set the problem aside and engage in some other activity. During this period of rest, your brain may actually end up giving you an answer to your question. This is how the incubation method works.

5. Each person also has to have proper ideas about concepts. Concepts encompass a lot of ideas, objects, or events. Concept formation has to begin in the early years. Language development is just as crucial. Thinking depends upon language and how the person is able to articulate their thoughts. Language can be in written or spoken form, but everyone has to have a good handle on it. All the words, symbols, signs, etc. used to act as tools during the thought process, if a

person's language development is insufficient, they cannot move towards effective thinking. Development of concepts and language is required for an efficient thought process. Improper development of these can hamper the person's progress and cause many issues that can affect their lives.

6. The reasoning process that a person adopts influences his thinking. Incorrect thoughts arise from illogical reasoning. Cultivating the habit of logical reasoning is important. Logic will help the person reason and think correctly.

Thinking tools

Thinking tools are some of the elements that are used in the thinking process:

1. Images of people, objects, situations, etc. can all be developed in mind. Mental images are manipulated by the way a person thinks. They symbolize real-life situations or things.

Thinking allows you to manipulate these mental images.

2. Concepts are general ideas of all objects or events in a general class. A concept can be used to economize the effort of thinking about something. If you hear of a single word, you will think of what that thing really is but also think about your experiences or how it is associated with you personally.

3. Symbols or signs are also tools used to represent objects, activities, etc. There are symbols all around us that we use to represent certain things generally. Such symbolic expressions then stimulate your thoughts and result in you deciding how to act accordingly.

4. One of the most effective tools for thinking is language. It is the most highly developed instrument that allows people to carry out their thought process. Any language that a person learns helps them to listen, speak or read in it. This stimulates their thinking and development through it. This is why reading

or writing acts as stimulants of the thinking process.

5. Taking part in activities that require muscle movement can also be helpful. There is a positive relation between thinking and muscular activities. Greater muscle tension is related to the more intensive thought process, and it applies conversely as well.

6. The main function of the brain is to think. This is why the mind is said to be the core tool of the thought process. Any experiences that our sense organs go through cannot be stimulating or work for our thought process unless the brain cells receive the signals and interpret them. Every mental image can only be used after the brain processes it and only then can you reconstruct them. The functioning of your brain is responsible for most of your thought process, and it would not be possible without the brain.

Automatic Intrusive Thoughts

Thoughts come in and go out of our mind all the time. These thoughts might be utterly unrelated to what you are doing at the time or where you are. You could be thinking about what you ate for lunch during class. Such random thoughts can occur in any unrelated situations. These types of thoughts can be of two types. One is like the above that is harmless and has no negative impact on you. The second instance is when the thoughts are negative and might incite maladaptive behavior. Automatic and intrusive thoughts are those that seem to suddenly come into your mind from nowhere. These kinds of thoughts can cause a surge of many different emotions like fear or sadness in the person. It can cause you to worry about things that have not happened yet or might never even happen, but you will still keep thinking about it. It can also make you think of a situation that might occur in the future, but you feel extremely grief ridden in the present.

The point is, these thoughts are sudden and involuntary and can lead to undesirable behavior. Automatic intrusive thoughts are a part of how addicts might think. They might be clean for a while but the sudden thought that they can try one more time might come into their head. Giving in to these kinds of thoughts is the undesirable behavior that you need to avoid. For addicts, it can cause a relapse that can even be fatal. When these thoughts come into an addict's mind, they cannot seem to shake it off or think of something else.

There are many reasons for why these kinds of sudden thoughts pop into someone's mind. It can be due to any trigger that plays a part in their addiction or illness. For addicts, the trigger could be a situation that prompts them to escape from reality. It could also just be the sight of someone related to his or her life of drugs. Sometimes, these thoughts pop back in your head just because you are trying too hard to suppress or ignore them.

If the thought of someone close to you dying keeps popping in your head, it will make you very sad every time. Some people are extremely sensitive and cannot process these kinds of thoughts or push them away. They might start crying right then even though the other person is living a perfectly healthy life at the time. But the thought of the loss that might come later seems too unbearable and they keep worrying about it.

As you can see, these sudden intrusive thoughts can have a very negative impact on your life. It is essential to identify these thoughts and deal with them before you act on the maladaptive reaction it could lead you to. Negative feelings are also in the stream of normal emotion, but they have to be in such a limit that you can process them healthily. If there are too many negative feelings in a person's mind, it can lead to unwanted behavior that could harm them or even another person. Instead of ignoring or trying to suppress such negative thoughts, you have to learn to process and deal with them. In this way, they will pass and not be stuck in your head. For instance, if a particular thought causes you to worry, analyze it. Think about the facts that are related to it; has it happened yet? Is there any indication that it is about to happen soon?

When you understand that there is no real need to worry, you can get rid of the thought and pacify your mind. You also need to learn to accept some things. For instance, the loss of a loved one who is old or incurably ill is inevitable. Worrying and obsessing over it will not change the situation. Grief is a normal emotion but let it come when it happens. Don't try to fight the inevitable and don't let these kinds of thoughts control you. Think of positive things when you feel such unnecessary negative thoughts popping up in your head. If something bad happens in the morning, don't keep thinking that the whole day is going to be bad. Just let go of it and try to go through the rest of the day typically. Holding on to negativity is counterproductive to your mental health.

Although it is easy to say such things, we know that it is harder to put them in practice. Learning to manage these intrusive thoughts is a process that takes time, but it will benefit you in the long run. It is essential to make an effort and not let negative emotions control and overtake our minds. Sometimes these thoughts can be extremely out of control, and that is where therapists can help you out. They can study and diagnose your problem and help in healing your mind. Intrusive thoughts can be a symptom of extreme distress or anxiety and need to be given due attention.

The process of thinking, reasoning or problem-solving in each person is affected by various factors. It is influenced by your habit of perceiving certain situations. Every person's experiences and perceptions from the past set a path for their way of thinking. This is why we can sometimes make mistakes in our conclusions when our thoughts are biased due to any likes, dislikes, prejudices, etc. The set way of thinking influenced by the past can hinder correct and effective thinking and lead to ineffective behavior.

If your thinking is not based on the information, then it can be incorrect and even harmful. Biases or prejudices do not allow you to be logical in your reasoning process. You can easily draw wrong conclusions when your thinking is based on these factors. It makes you ignore facts that support the right solution and instead reach the wrong conclusion. There are many reasons that can lead to errors in thought. When we let ourselves get swayed by our emotions, it can affect our thinking. For instance, fear of failure can affect a person's performance in an exam. Incorrect thinking also results from the inability to look at a problem from different angles. A broad viewpoint is needed to take everything into account.

Superstitions and a set belief system also affect your way of thinking. If you depend on these and not accurate information, then it will inadvertently lead to the wrong results or conclusions. This will be inhibitory to your growth process and the development of your thinking process. Unscientific thinking can cause a conflict of interest with facts and the truth. Wishful thinking or delusions can result in errors of thought as well. These kinds of thoughts can be dangerous or even fatal.

The Voices in your Head

Every time you are about to do something, does it feel like a voice in your head stops you from doing it? Does it feel like there is a constant war going on between you and the voice in your head? Here we will talk about these and how you can stop yourself from becoming a victim to these.

Most people with mental issues suffer a lot due to negative thinking. Negative thoughts lie at the core of so many issues that can easily be dealt with otherwise. In reality, negative thinking is wired into your brain to let you decipher what is wrong and protect yourself; it is a survival tool. But when these negative thoughts get out of control, they can create a different reality and don't just help you differentiate situations. People who have anxiety or suffer from depression are a prime example of this.

Someone who is depressed always has a focus on what is wrong in their lives or their past. They feel ashamed or guilty for what they may have done. Anxiety causes some people to fear what hasn't even happened yet. Both of these are a negative type of focus of thoughts. Chronic negative thinking causes depression and can make you numb to everything and all emotions including love or fear. There are negative voices in your head, which hold you back and don't allow you to progress in life. It is important to fight those voices and manage them before they take control of your life.

One of the common voices in a depressed person's head tells them that they don't deserve to be loved. This voice can stem from different incidents like a breakup. It makes you think that the breakup happened because of you and you keep blaming yourself. This same voice will create a pattern of thought that makes you feel unloved and undeserving of love at all times. It will give you illogical reasoning and convince you in a way that your self-esteem takes a huge hit, and you believe this voice blindly. If you listen to this voice for too long, it will cause you stop taking care of yourself, and you won't let others do it either. This pattern can lead to substance abuse where the person seeks solace from their emotions. This type of thinking can often result in people staying stuck in bad relationships. Even when they get out of one bad one, they enter another and reason that they deserve it or convince themselves that they don't deserve something better. You need to fight back this belief by using positive affirmations and telling yourself that you deserve love just like every other person in the world. Before focusing on giving love to others, you have to push away that voice in your head and learn to love yourself and receive it as well. Take care of yourself in every way possible and show yourself some self-love.

Another negative voice that gets stuck in the head of many people is the voice of regret. They are stuck in their past and what they failed to achieve at some point. They keep holding on to the regret of things they did not do or did do. These thoughts keep coming into their mind, and it keeps them stuck in an unproductive cycle. If you keep listening to the voice of regret, then you give it power over you to stop you from doing better in your present. You have to accept regret as an emotion, and it has to pass. You cannot hold on to it and obsess over it forever. You might regret that one thing but holding on to regret will lead to many more regrets down the line. Instead, use reaffirmation to tell yourself that you need to trust the process, and something good will come out of it all. Instead of wallowing in regret, you can think about what it is you regret and maybe try to correct the situation now. Identify the goal you wanted to achieve and try to achieve it now if you regretted not doing it earlier. If you regret the way you behaved towards someone, apologize to them and make sure you don't do it again. Don't keep regretting and punishing yourself. Transform the negative thoughts into a positive reality.

Another voice that gets stuck in your head may tell you that you are not ready for something that you really want or need to do. You need to realize that you or anyone else is never 100% ready for all the things that they go through in life. If it is something that you want to do, just go for it. Don't overthink or talk yourself out of it. That voice in your head has probably been telling you that you are not ready for a long time now, but you are. The results can be good or bad, but you will never know unless you try. Waiting for the right moment will just keep you stuck in a loop where you never get things done. Opportunities will not always come by. If you let them pass by you, at some point, you will see that you have lost all your chances. That little voice in your head will not help you, and it will turn into a voice of regret that will keep gnawing at you. Even if you don't feel you are half as ready as you should be, fight with the percentage that works in your favor. There will be many decisions in your life that you will have to make in the spur of the moment. You won't always get the chance to think them through or analyze them. You have to trust your gut and make some spur of the moment decisions and just pray things to work out. More often than not, you will see that they turn out okay. It might not be perfect but okay is also good. Getting out there will help in cultivating more experiences and build your character. Stopping yourself from doing things on the basis of fear and a negative voice in your head will get you nowhere. Use an affirmation thought telling yourself that you are ready and enough at every point in your life. You need to build your self-confidence in order to stand strong and face things head-on. You can always grow as a person, but you have what it takes to get there so don't doubt it. If you don't trust yourself, how can others have confidence in you either?

How changing your thought process can change your life

Changing your thoughts can accordingly help to change your life. It might sound far-fetched but trust us when we say it is true. Negative thoughts will result in negative energy in your life. It will cause you to stay stuck in a rut where you can't get things done and are not happy. Negative thoughts will hinder your growth as a person and cause problems like anxiety, depression, etc. Positive thoughts have the opposite effect and are obviously a power tool. However, you will be surprised with how most people allow negative thoughts to control them instead of positive thoughts that will benefit them.

You can take advantage of the fact that thoughts can change your life for the better. Your thought process plays a crucial role in who you are, what you do, what happens around you, etc. You can improve it for the better to see positive changes in your life. Constantly thinking about problems will stop you from making use of all the opportunities that come your way and can actually help you solve your problems. Focusing on problems makes you think you are doomed for failure and you might not even try hard enough to deal with them. You will tend to avoid action or introspection of these situations. The negative thoughts will thus be mirrored in your actual life.

If you learn to control these negative thoughts, you can take a step in the right direction. You can start focusing on success and what you need to do to achieve it. Think about what you want from your life and focus on that. Don't think about what has gone wrong and how things never seem to work out for you. These kinds of thoughts will work as a negative reaffirmation and just make things worse. Positive affirmations will help things work out in a positive way.

Creating a mental image of what you want and who you want to be can be a useful tool. This allows you to envision the possibilities of what you can achieve and gives you a goal to work towards. Having no aim can make you wander aimlessly and allows your mind to tend towards negative, useless thoughts freely. Thinking about failures and hardships all the time just closes doors of opportunity for you. Instead, think of success and happiness, and you will be motivated to achieve them. Open yourself to more possibilities and take advantage of all the chances you get to change your life for the better. If you have financial issues and keep focusing on how difficult your life is, you are just wasting time and energy that you can use to earn real money. You are just wasting time by thinking of how hard your life is and keep reaffirming that you will stay in that same situation. Instead, if you clear your mind of these thoughts, you can focus on changing your situation. A successful person will be using their time and energy to set goals and get past any obstacles in their way. They don't sit and lament about all the hardships they might have to face on the way. They focus and believe that they will fulfill their ambitions.

Thoughts and perseverance can help anyone achieve what they want. You should try reading more about the law of attraction to understand that what you are is what you will attract. If you are a negative person, you will only attract negative outcomes in your life. If you are a good and positive person, you will automatically attract goodness in your life. Learn more about how you can use creative visualization to envision and achieve goals. Perseverance is the key to achieving anything. The process of changing your thoughts will not be an easy one either, but you need to decide on what you want and work towards it. If you expect quick results, you will usually just give up even before you get a chance to really begin. There are no shortcuts to great things, but the effort will get you there. If you really want changes in your life you have to invest the time and effort into it. Just reading all this alone will not be enough; you have to use the right techniques to change your mindset and also take the right actions. This way you will work towards improving yourself and your life for the better. Complaining and thinking negative thoughts will keep you in the same situations for a long time and prevent you from making any progress in your life.

If you want to change your life, you have to change your thoughts. Changing how you think will help to change how you feel and how you react to situations. It will have an impact on the actions you take. This inner change of positive thinking will result in positive changes in your external life as well.

Chapter 2

What is Cognitive Behavioral Therapy?

In this chapter, we will explain what Cognitive behavioral therapy is and why people use it, and how they benefit from it. Cognitive behavioral therapy or CBT is a treatment pattern that aims to cure the effects of depression or any mental illness and also find a permanent solution by studying behavior or thinking patterns.

The main idea behind this therapy is that nearly all our actions have some thought process underlying them. Originally, CBT was designed to treat depression specifically, but over the years, it has been used expansively to treat many different kinds of mental health issues. The therapy is a type of psychosocial intervention that focuses on changing any negative behavior, thoughts or beliefs, improve emotional processing, and developing coping strategies.

The basic principles of behavioral as well as cognitive psychology are used in cognitive behavioral therapy. CBT focuses on problems and is oriented towards actions. It falls in the second wave of therapy and is different from the older approaches towards psychotherapy. Earlier, therapists used to study a person's behavior and look for the unconscious meaning behind them to diagnose the problem. CBT therapists are more focused on treating specific problems related to the mental disorder that a patient has been diagnosed with. They try to help the patient reach some goals using effective strategies that will help them and decrease their symptoms.

According to CBT, psychological disorders are related to thought distortions and maladaptive behavior. Teaching the patient coping mechanisms and other skills can reduce the symptoms and effects of the diagnosed diseases. One area of CBT was focused on changing maladaptive thinking to change the related behavior or effect on the patient. The other area that is more focused on these days emphasizes changing the patient's relationship with maladaptive thinking. CBT is not focused on diagnosing the patient and his disease but on finding as much of a solution as possible to benefit the patient.

Many studies have found that even without psychoactive medications, CBT is quite effective in treating milder forms of addictions, personality disorders, stress, depression, and anxiety. Therefore, doctors recommend a combination of medication with CBT to deal with more severe forms of these mental issues. Conditions like bipolar disorder, obsessive-compulsive disorder, major depression, etc. are treated using a combination of psychoactive medicines and CBT. Even children or adults with behavioral problems like aggression are recommended CBT to improve their behavior. Interpersonal psychotherapy and cognitive behavioral therapy are the only two psychosocial therapies that are compulsory for all psychiatry residents to train in.

Cognitive behavioral therapy involves cognitive therapy and behavior therapy. Let's try to understand these two types of individually.

Cognitive therapy

Aaron T. Beck was an American psychiatrist who first developed cognitive therapy. According to him a person's thoughts, feelings, and behavior are somehow interconnected to each other. Studying each of these aspects individually would not be an effective method of understanding a person's mental state accurately. Beck suggested the combined study of all three aspects to understand and diagnose a patient's condition. The appropriate treatment can be suggested only once this is done.

Behavior therapy

A person's state of mind is understood by studying their behavioral patterns. Using this information, the appropriate treatment is suggested. The purpose of behavior therapy is to treat a person by studying how they behave in different situations and respond to different stimuli. Sometimes their thoughts and feelings are also given attention to in this therapy, but the main focus is on actual behavior. The therapist subjects the person to all the situations that the patient would normally go through every day and studies their responses. They use this to try and understand what the cause of the problem is and try to solve it or find a way to deal with it for the patient.

Blending cognitive and behavior therapy is one of the best ways to treat patients using cognitive behavioral therapy. Using two different medical therapies properly together is much more beneficial for the patient. CBT emphasizes that logic or reason cannot be used to treat every disorder that affects the human mind. Sometimes you have to consider factors that defy logic as well. Medication can only go till a certain level. CBT and other therapies help in going the extra mile for proper treatment.

How to go about getting CBT?

When a person chooses to undergo CBT, a therapist will be assigned to that individual. A relationship needs to be established between these two people so that the patient can trust and allow the therapist to treat him appropriately. The therapist has to come in close contact with the person to understand his thoughts and behavior. They have to watch the person in their usual environment to study them properly. Regular sessions are conducted to allow the person to share their emotions and experiences with the therapist. You can go at your own pace as you choose to slowly open up to the therapist.

The therapy is taken step by step and allows the therapist to understand your mental state. CBT is a more direct approach than many other therapies and thus has better results. It focuses on the individual, and the treatment is more tailored according to their needs. The practical aspect of this therapy makes it much more effective than most methods used for mental health treatment.

There are six phases in mainstream CBT, and they are as follows:

- The first phase is the psychological assessment.
- The second phase is the reconceptualization.
- The third phase is skill acquisition.
- The fourth phase is the consolidation of skills and application training.

- The fifth phase involves generalization and maintenance.
- The final phase is the follow up on post-treatment assessment.

Kanfer and Saslow created these steps in a system for CBT. After the treatment is complete, the psychologist must assess if it worked for the patient or not. The decrease in the negatively-inclined behavior means that it was successful, but if it remains the same or their condition is aggravated, then the treatment failed.

CBT can be done in a group as well as individual settings. The term itself can refer to different types of interventions like goal setting, self-instruction, biofeedback, etc. Most of the techniques are adapted in a way that they can be applied for self-help. Some therapists may be more cognitively oriented while others will focus on behavioral therapy, but the entire process will include both.

History of CBT

Cognitive behavioral therapy has aspects that originated in different ancient philosophical traditions. Stoicism, in particular, is one from which CBT borrows its principles. Stoicism emphasized that any false beliefs that caused destructive emotions could be discarded by applying logic. This is the same as identifying cognitive distortions and treating them. Aaron T. Beck also referred to the origin of these thoughts in Stoic philosophy. Albert Ellis, John Stuart Mill, and Beck were some of the original endorsers of CBT for treatment of mental issues. Alfred Adler was one of the earliest therapists to talk of cognition in the field of psychotherapy. Albert Ellis was influenced by Adler's work and developed the REBT or rational emotive behavior therapy which is the earliest psychotherapy based on cognition. During this time, Aaron T. Beck started noticing that Freud's theory was not always applicable, and emotional distress could be the result of certain types of thoughts. He developed cognitive therapy from this and referred to such thoughts as automatic thoughts.

John B. Watson and Rayner conducted studies on conditioning around 1920, which were groundbreaking for behaviorism. Cognitive therapy developed around 1960, and behavior therapy can be traced to the early 1900s. Mary Cover Jones used behavioral therapy to study children in 1924. Joseph Wolfe further developed behavioral therapy in the 1950s using all these previously conducted studies. There were many more over the years who studied conditioning and behavior therapy, like Arnold Lazarus, Glenn Wilson, and Ivan Pavlov.

The theory put forward by John B. Watson, Clark L. Hull, and Ivan Pavlov inspired more study on the subject, and many researchers started using it in the United States, South Africa as well as the United Kingdom. Joseph Wolfe of Britain used behavioral research to treat neurotic disorders. His work was the early foundation of the fear reduction techniques that are used in the modern day.

Hans Eysenck promoted behavior therapy as an effective treatment, and at the same time, B.F. Skinner was working on operant conditioning. Later, Julian Rotter and Albert Bandura contributed with their work on social learning theory, and they demonstrated how cognition affects learning as well and behavior modification. The first wave of CBT was the emphasis on behavioral factors. The second wave was started by the REMT and cognitive therapy developed by Ellis and Beck.

The third wave of CBT developed from blending theory and technical applications of behavior therapy and cognitive therapy. Dialectical behavior therapy, acceptance, and commitment therapy are the most important therapies from the third wave of CBT.

Types of CBT

Let's take a look at the different types of cognitive behavioral therapy.

Brief cognitive behavioral therapy or BCBT

This is a form of CBT that was developed to deal with therapy that had time constraints. Usually, when BCBT is used for treatment, it takes around a total of 12 hours divided into a few sessions. David M. Rudd developed and implemented this technique to treat suicidal tendency in soldiers who were deployed overseas.

The first part of it is an orientation that involves a commitment to treatment, crisis response, safety planning, survival kits, reasons for the living card, a model of suicidal tendencies, treatment journal, means restriction, and lessons learned. The skill focus is on skill development worksheets, coping cards, demonstration, practice and, skill refinement. The third part is relapse prevention, which involves skill generalization and skill refinement.

Cognitive-emotional behavioral therapy or CEBT

CEBT was initially developed to treat those with eating disorders, but now it is used to treat many other problems like depression, PTSD, or even anger problems. CEBT uses dialectical behavioral therapy and cognitive behavioral therapy to help in understanding emotions and increase tolerance. This helps in the therapy and is often referred to as a pre-treatment for long-term therapy.

Structure cognitive behavioral training or SCBT

SCBT was developed with philosophies drawn from Cognitive behavior. It emphasizes that beliefs, emotions, and thoughts all are related to behavior. It also used Ellis's rational emotive behavior therapy and others to build on CBT. The only ways it is different from core CBT is that it has a much-regimented format, and it is a predetermined finite process. SCBT only becomes personalized from the input of the patient. This therapy was designed for getting specific results in limited time and has been used to treat addictive behavior related to substance abuse. Criminal psychology uses SCBT for recidivism reduction.

Moral reconation therapy

This therapy was developed to help treat antisocial personality disorder in felons. This helps in reducing the risk of them repeating their offenses in the future. Instead of one-on-one sessions, this therapy is conducted in groups. This is because it might otherwise reinforce narcissism in some felons. The group meetings are usually held once a week for about six months.

Stress inoculation training

This therapy is used to focus on stressors that affect patients. It uses cognitive and behavioral therapy with humanistic training for a blend that will benefit the patient. This therapy helps in coping with stress or anxiety issues and is a three-phase program. This therapy helps the individual to use their skills to adapt to the stressors.

The first phase of this therapy includes reading materials, psychological testing, and self-monitoring. This part of the process helps the therapist to create a program specifically for the individual. The second phase focuses on skills acquisition and continued conceptualization. Skills are taught to help the individual in dealing with the stressors that affect them and then these are practiced. It involves problem solving, communication, self-regulation, etc. The third phase involves a follow-through of the skills that were acquired in training. The individual gets the chance to use their skills on different stressors through role-play, imagery, etc. By the end of the training, the person will know how to break down their stressors and deal with them in the short term or long-term basis using their skills.

Mindfulness-based cognitive behavioral therapy

This therapy focuses on addressing subconscious tendencies and increasing awareness through a reflective approach. Three phases are used to achieve any goals that the individual sets.

Unified protocol

It is a form of the CBT that was developed at Boston University and is used to treat many depression and anxiety issues in patients, the unified protocol for trans-diagnostic treatment of emotional disorders gives the rationale that common underlying causes lead to most anxiety or depression disorders, and so they can be treated together. It involves psycho-education, cognitive reappraisal, emotion regulation, and changing behavior.

Pros and Cons of CBT

Just like everything else, CBT therapy has its pros and cons. The therapy can be found to be effective for many people but isn't necessarily suitable for all. Let's take a look at the disadvantages and advantages of cognitive behavioral therapy.

Pros:

- There are some mental illnesses where medication alone is not sufficient for treatment. CBT has been found to be helpful here, and along with medication, it helps in better treatment for the patient.
- If you compare CBT to other talking therapies, it is completed in a much shorter period of time which is an advantage.
- CBT is a very structured type of therapy, and this means that it can be provided through different means like books, apps, and one on one sessions or group therapy.
- It teaches strategies that are practical and can be used in everyday life even after the therapy is completed.

Cons:

- The therapy will not work unless the patient cooperates with the therapist. The therapist can only advise and help to a limit, after that your effort is necessary.
- It can take a lot of your time to attend the therapy sessions and also carry out the exercises in between sessions recommended by the therapist.
- The therapy may not be suitable for those who have special needs and learning difficulties.
- It might make you uncomfortable since you have to confront anxieties and emotions that make you uncomfortable.
- It focuses singularly on the person's capability to change their thoughts and behavior. It does not factor-in or work on external factors like other people who affect a person's mental health.
- It can also be a problem when CBT does not address issues of the past that deserve attention. This is because the therapy is too focused on the present.

Differences between CBT and other psychotherapies:

There are a few noticeable differences between this therapy and other psychotherapies that are practiced while treating mental health issues:

CBT is pragmatic and identifies specific problems and allows the patient to solve them on their own.

CBT is much more structured than other psychotherapies, which allow the patient to freely discuss their life and thoughts. CBT is focused on specific problems and goals.

Other therapies often involve discussion and analysis of past experiences to help the patient. CBT disregards the past and focuses only on current problems faced by the patient.

Other therapists might tell you what to do, and you would have to follow their instructions blindly. CBT is more of teamwork between the patient and the therapist, so they need to work together to find the solutions.

Chapter 3

Cognitive Distortion Awareness

In this chapter, we will learn about cognitive disorders, their symptoms, the effects of these disorders, and the most common cognitive distortion.

What are cognitive disorders?

Disorders that affect a person's cognitive abilities such as learning or memory are called cognitive disorders. These disorders can affect the cognitive function of the person in a way that it impairs their ability to stay in a normal environment. Cognitive disorders usually begin slowly and are not that noticeable, but over time they can seriously affect the quality of life of the individual.

Understanding and identifying a cognitive disorder will help in reducing the symptoms and treating the condition. Dementia, amnesia, motor skill disorders, and developmental disorders are some of the common cognitive disorders seen in people. One of the more prominently affecting cognitive disorders is Alzheimer's disease that affects millions of people around the world.

A variety of factors can cause cognitive disorders in people. Some people acquire these through genetics while others may be affected due to hormonal imbalances while they were in the womb. Environmental factors also play a role in the development of cognitive disorders. This can be due to improper nutrition while the child is in the womb as well. Substance abuse is another cause along with physical injuries that can cause a cognitive disorder to develop. Cognitive dysfunction may result from damage to certain areas of the brain that are responsible for cognitive functions. This can be due to physical trauma or the effect of drugs and alcohol on the brain.

Symptoms of cognitive disorders

The signs of a cognitive disorder may vary according to the condition, but a few common symptoms are observed in most cases. Some of these include confusion, impaired judgment, and confusion about identity, motor coordination issues, or even loss of memory. The symptoms of a cognitive disorder can be subtle initially, but the severity increases over time with the progression of the disease. One of the prime examples of this is Alzheimer's disease where the patient starts becoming forgetful about small things during early onset.

As the disease progresses over time, the person's memory can become severely impaired. Initially, they forget a few names or what they did the previous day. Later, they fail to recognize their loved ones and lose track of time as well. They might have some moments of clarity where everything seems normal again, but these pass and a confused state persists. It is important to pay attention to the early symptoms to help the patient as much as possible in fighting such diseases.

Physical symptoms include lack of motor coordination and unusual mannerisms. The person will tend to look confused or dazed most of the time. You might notice abnormal posture or problems in the balance as well.

Other than the symptoms stated above, an emotional imbalance is also observed in cognitive disorders. People who suffer from these conditions are prone to getting frustrated and emotional outbursts. This kind of emotional imbalance can be hard for the people around them to deal with. While some people have aggravated emotions, others might become numb and act emotionless. The reactions can differ in people.

Effects of cognitive disorders

Cognitive dysfunctions can cause short-term as well as long-term effects. Short-term effects like memory loss or a confused state are common. Long-term effects include forgetfulness, emotional instability, loss of memory, lack of control, etc. All of these affect the way of life of a person suffering from cognitive disorders.

Treatment

Various options for treatment of cognitive issues are available. Most cognitive disorders cannot be treated permanently, but the quality of life can be improved using drugs and treatments. Many drugs or supplements have been generated to help patients deal with cognitive dysfunctions like memory loss. Associated issues like depression or anxiety can also be treated using antidepressants and other drugs. Antidepressants are one of the most commonly used drugs for people with cognitive disorders.

Drugs are also used to help retain memory as much as possible for the person. A medical assessment helps the doctor to prescribe the appropriate drugs for any patient. However, such medications also come with some side effects that need to be kept in mind. Side effects include drowsiness and insomnia. The doctor will usually keep a close eye to check the effects of a particular medication on an individual and determine if it is helping them.

Suffering from cognitive dysfunctions can be extremely hard for a person. It makes them frustrated and irritable when they realize how the disease is affecting their lives. It has a negative effect on their mental stability, and this can lead to maladaptive behavior. Some people may look for control over their situation through means like drugs or alcohol abuse. Because of the lack of control that comes with these conditions, patients look for a way to assert control-using drugs like stimulants that improve mental functioning.

Self-prescription of these doses is a common abuse. There are also cases of an overdose on such medications. Some patients increase the dosage by themselves if they feel like the prescribed dosage is not helping them. This can be quite dangerous and even fatal. Having too many of these drugs over time, the person can become dependent on these medications and even suffer from withdrawal symptoms when they try to get off them. Medical supervision is required to help patients recover from such symptoms.

Cognitive disorders are quite often linked with addictions in patients. Due to this, many types of research even say that addiction is a type of cognitive dysfunction. Substance abuse itself can be the cause of some types of cognitive impairments. ADHD is very commonly prevalent amongst alcoholics, and they are more prone to it.

Common cognitive distortions

Cognitive distortions are ways in which your mind may convince you of things that are not true. Inaccurate thoughts linked to negative thinking arise in your mind, and you feel like they are accurate and make sense. However, these are irrational thoughts that only make you feel bad about yourself. Such cognitive distortions play a major role in your behavior. It is important to identify these cognitive distortions to refute the negative thinking and replace it with more balanced thoughts.

Some of the more common cognitive distortions are as follows:

1. Mental filtering is one of the cognitive distortions that make a person focus on negative details and magnify them. Instead of focusing on reality, it allows the person to only see the negative aspect of everything and block out the positive
2. Another distortion is polarized thinking which makes the person feel like things either have to be perfect or totally wrong. This does not allow them to be satisfied with any gray area and accept that some things may go wrong. Thinking in black and white can make situations seem extreme.
3. Another problem is generalizing based on a single fact or an incident. The person may feel defeated with everything even if they fail at one single instance. For instance, a student failing one test will conclude that his whole semester will be bad and that he should just quit.
4. Jumping to conclusions can be another distorted behavior. The person might think

that another person is holding a grudge against them or hates them just because of a single unpleasant encounter. They might also conclude what their future will hold based on a single instance.

5. Some people tend to believe that something really bad will happen and it is inevitable. They will always assume the worst in a situation and believe that it will turn out badly.

6. Another distortive behavior is when the person takes everything personally. They always think that what another person does or says is somehow connected to them or directed towards them. They think of themselves as the center of everything and everyone's life around them.

7. Another distortion is where they feel like no one is fair to them. They often feel resentful and angry whenever things don't go their way.

8. Blaming others for what happens in your life or for your feelings is another type of distortive behavior. The situation could also

be reversed, and instead, they blame everything on themselves. There is no rationale for the reasoning behind all the blaming, but it is always focused in one direction in an unhealthy way.

9. Emotional reasoning is another tendency that can be problematic. The person believes that everything that they feel is valid and true. Emotions can be very strong and take over rational thinking. Emotional reasoning can be an unhealthy way of reflecting on situations.

10. Another distortive tendency is to expect changes in others according to what you think they need to change. This is commonly seen in relationships where one partner expects the other to change because they believe it is for their better and only then will they be perfect.

11. Labeling is another unhealthy habit that can be quite a hindrance. The person will generalize and label another person based on a single negative quality. It can also be applied to themselves where they generalize

themselves as a failure if they fail at one single thing. This kind of labeling can be very judgmental and offensive.

12. Some people also have the problem of thinking that they are always right and feel the need to prove that the other person is wrong. They do not consider that they can be wrong sometimes and go to huge lengths to emphasize that they are right. They usually disregard the truth or others' feelings and only righteously look at themselves.

Cognitive behavioral therapy alone with medications can help in the treatment of these distortive symptoms. It helps the patient identify their negative behavior and teaches them to improve their perspective. CBT also helps them in practicing more positive thoughts and improving their distortive symptoms.

Depression is linked to any cognitive symptoms like these. It makes the depressed person think negatively and associate every situation with a negative outcome. It is vital to teach these individuals to think more positively. They are first taught to monitor all negative thoughts using tools like a journal. Then they are taught to challenge and rationalize these thoughts to replace them with better thoughts. There are many steps involved, but ultimately treatment and medication can help improve distortive conditions to a noticeable extent.

Chapter 4

Cognitive Restructuring

Cognitive distortions are usually just like any bad habit, and they can be changed for the better with time and practice. An important part of CBT is cognitive restructuring. It is a process that teaches the individual to identify and refute all maladaptive thoughts. Strategies like thought recording, guided imagery, and Socratic questioning are used in cognitive restructuring. Some other commonly used methods include reattribution cognitive rehearsal and listing rational alternatives. The goal of cognitive restructuring is to help the individual change stressful thought patterns to a less stress-inducing way of thinking.

The cognitive restructuring was initially developed as a part of CBT and REBT. This technique has helped many people learn to cope better with stressful situations and thoughts. It is a little difficult to implement it by yourself, but with assistance from a therapist, the technique can be quite useful.

There are four steps involved in cognitive restructuring:

1. The first step is to identify any automatic intrusive thoughts that cause the person to think negatively.
2. The second step is to identify the cognitive distortions associated with these negative thoughts identified in step one.
3. The third step is to rationally dispute all such negative automatic thoughts.
4. The fourth step is to develop rational rebuttals of such thoughts.

Take some time and start noticing whenever you have any cognitive distortion. Take notice of any time where you find yourself thinking negatively and jumping to negative conclusions. Then ask yourself how you can change your view about that situation. Think of the positive outcomes possible instead of any negative outcome that you predicted. Think of what the most realistic outcome could be.

Use a journal to mark down every time you over-think a situation and write if those thoughts helped in solving any problem. Do these for a few days and at the end, check how many times the over-thinking helped you in any way. You should also start marking down your daily routine and rate your productivity level every day. Compare your productivity level every few weeks.

When you have a negative thought, evaluate it. Write down any evidence that supports the negative thought and write down what proves that you are wrong. Keep trying this to rationalize what thoughts are valid and true.

Mindfulness meditation also helps in focusing your attention to the present. Every time you think of something negative, try and bring your attention back to something like your breathing. You also need to reduce self-criticism and be more compassionate towards yourself. If you do something wrong or silly, talk kindly to yourself and acknowledge your wrongdoing as part of human experience. This will also help you to think more kindly about others over time.

Cognitive restricting will help you to learn how you can stop listening to your automatic thoughts and test them for accuracy. It involves evaluation of the thoughts that come into your mind and learning how to change them for the better. Asking yourself some questions will help you in the process. Think about any evidence that supports your thoughts and what doesn't. Question yourself to find out if you are underestimating yourself and your coping abilities. Think of the worst possible scenarios and compare them to your current situation.

After the process of cognitive restructuring, think of your original thoughts again and rephrase them to be more accurate and not distorted. With some practice and patience, you will be able to change all your stress-inducing thoughts and feel better.

Chapter 5

Depression & Anxiety

Depression

Do you often feel "down" or experience "the blues"? Most people talk about it casually and don't give much thought to this kind of feeling. You might think it is entirely normal and it is but to a limit. Your entire life will at some point or the other, cause you to encounter situations where you feel sad or rejected. Unrealistic expectations from the people around you will create a sense of disappointment and rejection that can sometimes be overwhelming. It is normal to feel sad about certain things for a while, but if you feel low most of the time, then you might be suffering from depression.

Depression makes you feel sad, lose interest in things, and feel low persistently as you go about your daily life. These are all feelings that everyone experiences, but if they persist for too long, it can affect your mental and physical health. Studies conducted have shown that nearly 8 percent of the population suffers from depression and this includes all people over 12. The scale somehow seems to be increasing over the years, but not enough attention is paid to mental health even now.

The World Health Organization stated that depression is the most common disease that ails people worldwide and at least 300 million people are affected by it all over the world. You might feel like you are alone or even be ashamed to admit this illness, but you have no cause to. It is actually more common than you realize and can be treated.

Depression is more common among women than it is among men. It makes you lose interest in things that you previously enjoyed, and you feel unable to find joy in anything at all. Depression is different from grieving like during the death of a loved one. Differentiating depression from mood fluctuations is crucial. A temporary response to a situation that makes you sad is not the same as being depressed. However, depression can result from the bereavement for a loved one. It is not easy to understand the real causes of depression, and there is no single reason. It involves genetic, environmental, biological, and psychological factors.

Depression is diagnosed by consulting a doctor or specialist. Seeking the help of a health professional for mental illness is just as important as it is for physical illness. Don't assume that you can work everything out on your own. You must reach out for help. A professional will evaluate your condition, find the cause, and recommend the best treatment for your benefit. The assessment can also include a physical medical check-up to rule out all possible causes that can be linked to your physical health as well. Doctors also use questionnaires to assess how severe the depression is and to learn more about the patient. One of the most commonly used tools for rating depression is the Hamilton scale.

Symptoms of depression

- Lack or reduction of interest in activities you previously loved.
- Slow movement and speech.
- Feeling low all the time.
- Abnormal sleeping patterns like insomnia or hypersomnia.
- Lack of energy or fatigue.
- Feeling guilty or worthless all the time.
- Lack of concentration.
- Inability to think clearly.
- Thoughts of suicide or death.
- Lack of appetite and weight loss.
- Lack of sexual desire.

Types of depression

Depression is quite difficult to endure, and it is a risk factor for several chronic conditions like heart diseases and dementia. Certain depressive symptoms can occur due to various reasons. If you or anyone you know is experiencing any mood swings or any cognitive changes for more than a couple of weeks, then it's a good idea to consult your medical practitioner about it. There are four common types of depression, and they are major depression, bipolar disorder, seasonal affective disorder, and persistent disorder.

Major depression is a classic type of depression. In this state, the mood of the person going through it will be quite dark and all-consuming. The individual might also lose interest in all activities including the ones that they used to enjoy. They may experience insomnia, difficulty in sleeping, weight loss, loss of appetite, and a general feeling of worthlessness. Thoughts of death, as well as suicide, are commonly reported. Psychotherapy and medication are the usual modes of treatment.

Dysthymia is now known as persistent depressive disorder. It refers to the sort of depression that's characterized by spells of low mood. It can last for as long as two years before it transforms into a major depression. People who are diagnosed with this form of depression are capable of going through their daily lives but tend to feel quite low and joyless most of the time. The other symptoms include loss of appetite, sleep changes, consistently low levels of energy and low self-esteem.

Bipolar disorder was originally known as manic-depressive disorder and those who suffer from this condition experience bouts of depression. Their mood oscillates between periods of happiness or exceptionally high energy and periods of absolute depression. The common symptoms that characterize this form of depression are quite the opposite those of general depression. The symptoms of bipolar disorder include grand ideas, unrealistic high self-esteem, reduction in the need for sleep, ability to process things at a great speed, indulging in activities to attain extreme pleasure and even overspending. Terrible bouts of depression follow spells of extreme happiness. A person having bipolar disorder can experience the highest of highs and the lowest of lows. Medication is the most effective way to treat this disorder.

The seasonal affective disorder usually occurs when the days tend to grow shorter like in autumn and winter. This change in mood seems to be the result of the alterations in the daily rhythms of the body, the sensitivity to light, or even the way in which serotonin and melatonin function in the body.

Causes of depression

No definitive cause can be explained as the reason for depression. It develops as a result of a combination of factors like genetics, environment, biological factors, and social factors. However, some people are more at risk due to specific reasons than others, such as:

- Issues with friends or family like divorce.
- Medical concerns like a chronic illness or stress.
- Death of a loved one.
- Personality traits like low self-esteem or lack of self-confidence. Less ability to successfully cope with situations.

- Experiencing a traumatic childhood or incident.
- Substance abuse like drug addiction, alcoholism, etc.
- Having relatives with depression.
- Prescription drug abuse.
- Chronic pain syndrome.
- Head injury in the past.

All of the above increase the risk of an individual to suffer from depression and should be kept in mind.

Treatments for depression

Three components are involved in treating depression. The first is getting support from family and everyone around you. Let your family know what you are suffering from and help them understand it. They will help and support you through the process. Also, seek the support of professionals for your treatment. The second phase involves undergoing psychotherapy using therapies like cognitive behavioral therapy. This will help to understand and alleviate the symptoms of depression. The third component involves antidepressant medicines to treat your condition.

Psychotherapy is used as the first option when the case is not too severe. Therapies like CT or interpersonal psychotherapy depression can be quite beneficial and effective for the patient. These are the two most commonly used treatments for treating depression. CBT can be used in one on one sessions or in a group depending on the individual and therapist.

Antidepressants are used when the depression is much more severe. At that point, psychotherapy alone is not enough. Drugs are not recommended for treating children with depression and are prescribed with caution. There are different classes of antidepressants that act on different neurotransmitters. It is important to use drugs only according to a doctor's prescription, or you can make your condition even worse. Continue the drugs even after you see improvement in your condition if your doctor recommends it. This is to prevent any chances of a relapse. The treatment of depression is a long process that you need to stay patient about. Always consult a doctor when you start or stop antidepressants.

Amongst other treatments, patients are advised to partake in some regular exercise to increase the endorphin levels in the body. This will stimulate the nor-epinephrine, which is a neurotransmitter that affects mood.

Brain stimulation therapies like electroconvulsive therapy are also used to treat depression.

Anxiety

Do you experience intense feelings of fear and worry? Even in everyday situations where you don't need to feel such persistent worry, you start breathing heavily and your heart rate increases. These are all signs of anxiety. In some stressful situations, anxiety can be a very normal reaction. Certain situations make most people uncomfortable when they are not used to them. However, if it becomes an all-consuming feeling in your daily life, there is reason to worry. Anxiety disorder can be a tough condition to live with. It overwhelms your mind and body and leaves you feeling tired. Thankfully, it can be treated just like depression. CBT is a useful type of psychotherapy to treat anxiety as well.

Some people suffer from extreme social anxiety, which usually makes them feel awkward and uncomfortable when there are a lot of people around them. They channel negative thoughts, causing them to feel like they are weird and inadequate. To push away these feelings, such people often resort to drinking or drugs. This maladaptive coping will only cause more problems and can prove to be fatal. CBT can help such anxiety disorders by teaching the person to refute such negative thoughts and develop more positive thinking. Healthy coping mechanisms are taught to reduce stress and help them feel calm in such anxiety-inducing situations. CBT has helped many people defeat anxiety disorders and lead a more normal life.

Causes of anxiety:

- Panic disorders lead to anxiety, heart palpitations and dizziness.
- Phobias.
- Stress factors like relationships, work, finances, etc.
- Anxiety also stems from having to deal with a medical illness that is chronic and takes a toll on ordinary life.
- Generalized anxiety disorder.
- Side effects of certain medications also cause anxiety.

Some skills from CBT used to combat anxiety are as follows:

- The person is taught to have more tolerance for uncertainty. Some people who are unable to deal with the uncertainty of a situation get anxious over it. Learning to accept and be more tolerant can be very beneficial.
- They are also taught to notice when they keep thinking the same worrisome thoughts again and again, but it does not help them.

Overthinking will reduce the ability to deal with a situation.

- They are also taught to recognize thought distortions like the prediction of adverse outcomes. The person has to identify such thoughts and rationalize them out. This way it can help them change the thoughts more positively.
- Anxiety can also be dealt with using mindfulness techniques. It helps to cope with the situation instead of avoiding it and also control over-thinking negative thoughts.

CBT works similarly for both anxiety and depression and helps the individual to lead a happier life.

Chapter 6

Journaling

Do you remember writing a diary as a kid or even when you are in high school? You probably gave the diary a name and treated it as your confidant. You could share whatever you did the whole day and your feelings about things without worrying about any judgment. You just had to write it all down and feel better. Most people grow out of this habit as they get older and become embarrassed to even put words to such thoughts in their head. There is a fear of someone else coming across such thoughts in your diary. This habit can be beneficial and should be continued. In psychology, it is called journaling.

Therapists recommend journaling to patients as a part of their therapy. You can write down your thoughts and feelings every day, and this will help you understand them better. Keeping a journal can also be very beneficial in the treatment of issues like depression, stress or anxiety. The process helps you see things more clearly and regain control of your emotions. It is always better to find an outlet for negative emotions rather than suppressing and keeping them in. A journal is one tool you can use for this purpose.

Effective journaling is a tool that can help an individual to set goals, meet them and improve the general quality of life. It can be different for different people, but the outcome is usually positive for everyone. There are many different reasons that make journaling effective. Writing can help you to clear your head, connect your thoughts and feelings and analyze them. It also helps you to deal with negative thoughts and turn them into positive ones.

You might be doubtful about how journaling benefits mental health but trust us when we say it does. Many therapists have used this as a tool, and a lot of research also supports this. This simple practice of writing down your feelings and thoughts helps in striving towards a healthy mindset. Journaling has helped people boost their mood, improve memory, feel better, reduce depression symptoms, and reduce automatic thoughts.

People with PTSD post-traumatic stress disorder have found journaling to be a very useful practice. The writing helps them to confront emotions that they might otherwise suppress. It helps them to process any difficult events they went through. As they write, they create a sort of narrative of events that helps to put things in perspective for them. The patient has to confront the events and emotions related to their trauma and thus deal with it. Suppressing and ignoring the situation is detrimental to health.

You do not need to suffer from PTSD to benefit from journaling. In general, it helps people to improve mental wellbeing. You become more aware of what you do and think and what happens around you as you journal. You can use the journal to analyze and detect unhealthy thought patterns and address them. It is important to identify cognitive distortions in behavior or thoughts to treat them. You then gain more control over your days and learn to shift from negativity to a more positive mindset. This applies to yourself and the people around you.

The journaling itself has to be done it the right manner to benefit you. Writing random things without any thought to it will not be very useful. For constructive journaling, you need to keep some things in mind. One aspect is that you should write in a space that is personal and free from any distractions. You need to write every single day and note down at least a few parts of each day. After you finish writing about your day, you need to give yourself a bit of time to reflect on it. This will help you to take notice of your train of thoughts and actions. You should also find a private place to store the journal so that you know no one else will be privy to it. The journaling is for your eyes and benefit. Keeping it secure will allow you to be more open in your writing. You can share the thoughts in your journal with your therapist, but you don't necessarily have to show it to them either. Don't feel obligated to share the journal with anyone else.

Things to keep in mind while journaling:

- Think about what you want to write in your journal. Write about what is going on in your life, what your goals are and what your thoughts are. Also, write about what you are trying to avoid or ignore as well.

- After you write you need to take some time to reflect on the entry. Stay calm and take a few breaths.
- Use your writing to understand your thoughts and feelings. Take time and stop if you feel like you don't know what to write. Take a breath and start again.
- Try to set some time aside to write every day. Make sure you stick to writing for that much time.
- After your done, take a moment to reflect on everything you wrote and understood from your entry. Sum up your experience for that day in a sentence or two. Try to think of how you can do better next time.

Tips for journaling:

These tips will help you get started with journaling.

- Try writing as soon as you wake up or right before you go to sleep.

- Always try to be honest to yourself in your journal. You don't need to hide anything or filter your thoughts because the journal is for your eyes only.
- To get started, describe what you did the whole day. You can write about what you saw, what you thought, and even what happened to others around you. There is never any lack of things to write about.
- When you want to deal with your negative feelings or feel like you need a boost, try affirmations. These are sentences that you use to write positive things about yourself, and they boost your self-esteem. You need to develop a healthy sense of self-worth.
- Try writing about the people or things in your life that you are grateful for. You can write about something good that happened that day and how grateful you were for it. It can be some kind words or a gesture of kindness from others or just anything that you are thankful for in general.
- Write about your dreams and goals and what you are doing to achieve them.

- Be your own critic in your journal but rationally and healthily. If you feel like you did something wrong, then analyze it and think of how you can do better.
- You can write about how you did at work or in any activity you took part in. Journaling can help you think about how you can do better and notice what you need to improve.
- You get a free zone to express your fears and anxiety. You can write about them and try to get to the source of this anxiety as well.
- Use your journal as a log of all the success you achieve. Mark down all the progress you make every day in dealing with your emotions, behavior and mental health.

A lot of research has shown that journaling is effective in helping people deal with stress, anxiety, and depression. It helps people with mental illness to identify their symptoms and accept their emotions. Journaling helps in easing the symptoms related to mental illness and improve quality of life. This simple practice also impacts the physical well being as it helps to deal with stress and related effects on the body. Also at the end of the day before going to bed, journaling will even help to improve your sleep cycle.

Does journaling help to treat depression?

The answer is definitely yes. It has been seen that journaling helps in managing symptoms of depression in people. Including journaling as a part of CBT helps to improve the results of the treatment. It is not effective singularly but combined with other tools for treatment, it is known to be very effective.

Studies have shown that writing has helped women who suffer from depression due to abusive relationships. It also helps adolescents who suffer from depression and are at risk for destructive behavior. Although journaling may not decrease how often automatic thoughts come into the mind, they help in limiting their impact. Journaling helps to reduce symptoms of depression like rumination as well. Research showed that those with major depression saw their depression scores lower within a few days of journaling. The overall benefit of journaling is quite clear. It allows you to release emotions, stay in a positive frame of mind, and build a buffer for negative thoughts.

Journaling can also help you through the process of recovery. If you have experienced a traumatic event, it can help to find good in every day. Writing your everyday experiences can make you find the positive aspects of your life and deal with the side effects of your trauma. For people that have eating disorders, it can be a relieving and healing method. It helps to limit obsessing over certain things and confront issues in a more head-on way. Journaling helps those with mental illnesses to stop ruminating and free their minds in a way that they can cope with the stress or anxiety bothering them. It can also help you to deal with the loss of a loved one. Expressing your emotions in a journal helps to process the loss and even prevent some maladaptive symptoms of coping that might arise. Children, who have to deal with bereavement, find this practice particularly helpful. The most important role in recovery played by journaling is in case of addiction. Addicts find that journaling helps them in their struggle against addiction. It allows them to also keep a record of their struggles as well as their accomplishments. They get a chance to hold themselves accountable for their actions and find a way to express their thoughts. The recovery from addiction can be a particularly hard process if the addict does not learn to control their thoughts and emotions healthily.

When you write down your thoughts and actions, it helps you to solidify your experiences and sense of self. You get a chance to reflect on what you have done and learn more about yourself every day. A journal allows you the chance to create a narrative for your own life. You realize that all the choices you make and your memories from the past together make you who you are. Journaling has a cathartic benefit on recovery.

Gratitude

One of the tools, which you can use while journaling, is cultivating gratitude. Gratitude is a very positive practice and is effective in helping people reach their goals as well as improving their life. Writing is one of the easiest ways to express gratitude.

- Gratitude helps to improve your well being in the long term.
- It helps to improve the quality of your sleep cycles.
- It helps in making you more optimistic and focuses on health and happiness.
- Gratitude journaling is effective in treating depression symptoms.
- Gratitude helps in improving your attitude towards people and life in general. Instead of antisocial tendencies, it promotes pro-social behavior.

Benefits of journaling:

If your in need of further convincing about the benefits of journaling, these will help you:

1. Journaling encourages and improves creative abilities.
2. It helps you to set goals and bring them to life.

3. It allows you the chance to get relief from stressors and let go of things that are not important.
4. It helps you to identify and explore your emotions or feelings.
5. You get a chance to write down the pros and cons of certain actions or decisions, helping you to reduce stress in your life
6. You will learn to pay attention to things that you previously might have ignored. This includes patterns of negativity in your behavior or thinking.
7. You will notice what factors influence your thoughts and actions every day.
8. Journaling allows you to channel all your emotions into words and thus release tension that can get pent up without expression.
9. Journaling can help you to discover your voice and improve writing skills.
10. You get a chance to keep a written record of your life that will be one of your precious keepsakes in the future.

11. You will see an increase in the sense of gratitude and learn to appreciate the good things in your life.

Precautions while journaling:

- Although journaling is a very helpful practice, don't think about it too much.
- Don't let the practice of writing about your life make you a passive observer of it.
- Don't use it to blame yourself for everything that happens. The aim is to find solutions to problems and not blame.
- Don't let it be a self-obsessive practice of writing about yourself.
- Don't focus on all the negativity in your life in your journal.

I hope all this information helps you to understand the benefits of journaling and encourages you to try it alongside your CBT therapy. If it is practiced the right way, it can lead to positive outcomes in your life and for your mental health. Don't let your journaling become an escape from the real world and start focusing on it obsessively.

Use it as a reflective tool that allows you to record your days and emotions. The benefits of journaling are far more than any disadvantages the practice could have. Use the tips given above to go about it the right way. You will see that it helps a lot in reducing stress and anxiety from your daily life.

Chapter 7

Mindfulness Meditation

Mindfulness meditation is yet another practice that is found to help in the treatment of mental illness along with CBT. It works as an additional tool that helps the individual improve the quality of their lives and attain real mental peace. The practice of meditation has been carried out for centuries and for good reason.

Mindfulness meditation is a type of training that teaches your mind to focus on what you are experiencing in the present moment. Instead of thinking of the past or future, you learn to live in the present. It teaches you to block out all the unnecessary chatter around you and also inside your mind. You learn to focus on things that matter singularly. This mental training practice involves breathing exercises, imagery, relaxation of the body and mind, and increased awareness as well.

The purpose of mindfulness meditation is to teach the individual to be more present in the now and increase awareness. The practice helps in the treatment of stress, anxiety, depression, insomnia, and other mental health issues. There are many ways to learn this practice. You can do it yourself through self-help programs or find a teacher to guide you. It is quite simple and can easily be included in your everyday routine. A few minutes every day to start with will make a difference.

- Start with finding a quiet and distraction-free area in your home.
- Sit in a comfortable but straight posture. Don't be stiff.
- Put aside thoughts of the past or future. Focus on the present.
- Start paying attention to your breathing. Focus on the movement of inhaling and exhaling. Notice how the air enters through your nose and let it out through your mouth.

Practice this breathing exercise and focus on it.

- Don't try to control the thoughts that come into your head. Let them come and go. You don't have to think about them or ignore them. Just be a bystander and watch these thoughts pass as you keep breathing.
- If you start getting distracted to think of something else, slowly bring your focus back to your breathing. Don't get anxious about the distraction, notice it but come back from it.
- Meditate for as long as you want to or can. Before you get up, slowly bring your focus to the present surroundings.

This meditation practice has many advantages for your mental as well as physical wellbeing. However, there is no mandatory guideline for instilling this into our life. You can meditate in an open park if you don't want to sit in the corner of your house. You also don't have to sit and meditate as we explained. You can choose to find some time that will allow you to be alone with your thoughts without being disturbed. In all the daily activities that you perform every day, it is easy to multitask and use this time for some mindfulness.

Try to Pay attention to the task you are performing, how you are feeling and the ground beneath your feet. This can be while you brush your teeth or even clean your house. Instead of watching videos while exercising, use this time to quietly move. Pay close attention to your movements and your breath and how your body feels. Turn off any sounds around you. These are simple ways to include mindfulness in your activities.

Mindfulness-integrated Cognitive Behavior Therapy

Let us now look at the application of mindfulness in CBT. You now have a simple idea of what mindfulness is and how you can implement it in your daily life. Here you will learn how it helps in the treatment of mental conditions along with CBT. Many psychological disorders can be treated using mindfulness integrated cognitive behavior therapy or MCBT.

It teaches you to pay attention to everything going on in your mind and around you in the present without being judgmental. You learn to be accepting and not react to every single thing that happens unless you need to. Mindfulness helps in countering the effects of stress or anxiety and helps you get detached to an extent. MCBT aims to help you see things as they are. Mindfulness also teaches you the reality of impermanence. You learn to accept that everything changes including your thoughts. It helps you to detach yourself from any bad habits or rigid views. These can cause unhappiness in your life, but mindfulness helps you detach from these elements.

MCBT involves four steps in its therapeutic approach to heal people. It integrates mindfulness with the principles of CBT to improve the way people think and behave. The approach is just a little different from what normal CBT entails. MCBT can help people in learning how to control the processes that cause unrealistic thoughts or beliefs in their minds. CBT by itself tries to change the behavior by changing the thoughts and beliefs. The process of thinking itself is changed using MCBT.

1. The first stage teaches mindfulness skills that help you to take note of unhelpful thoughts or emotions and let go of them. This is done for the person to successfully deal with the challenges life throws at them. The first stage of MCBT will teach you equanimity and help in developing deep insight so that you don't fall prey to all the negative thoughts that enter your mind.
2. The second stage allows you to implement the skills taught in the first stage. You will have to face situations that you would probably avoid normally, and this will help in increasing your confidence levels.
3. The third stage teaches you to improve interpersonal understanding and develop better communication skills. This will help you in situations where you might normally feel tense or cornered. You will learn not to react just because someone provokes you either.
4. The fourth stage teaches you to empathize with yourself. You need to learn to be kind to yourself and also to others. This empathy has

to be visible in what you do every day. It will improve your sense of worthiness and also improve your relationship with others. It is important to develop a caring nature and connect with others.

MCBT also helps in changing unhelpful coping strategies by using exposure as well as desensitization principles. According to the principles of this therapy, the reactive habits of a person are due to their reaction habits to body sensations. These body sensations develop from the way we think and learn to react to certain sensations to feel better. These habits usually develop since an early age and stick, as we grow older. MCBT helps in preventing these conditioned reactions but increasing awareness and acceptance of these experiences. This helps in changing habitual behavior and even feelings that arise in us. Thus, the therapy helps in providing emotional relief.

Other than changing their thoughts and behavior, MCBT also helps people to improve their relationships with those around them. It helps them to be more compassionate and accepting of others as they learn to be kinder to themselves. This helps in the development of harmonious relationships with people who will support and help you from relapsing into negativity again. The third phase of the therapy deals with this aspect of interpersonal mindfulness. The fourth stage teaches people to make use of the skills they learn and empathize with others as well as themselves. The last stage of the process sees the person become much more empowered and accepting of their emotions, situations, and the people around them. The duration of the entire program will depend on the individual and their needs.

Chapter 8

Dealing with Negative Thinking and Self-Talk

Negative thinking causes people to anticipate the absolute worst in every situation or circumstance. The negative thoughts that rooted from this type of thinking are not favorable for what that person needs or wants. Such people think of the negative aspect of everything. For instance, even if they like dogs, they think about the mess they would make and decide not to keep one. They know that a dog is loving and would make them happy, but they ignore this positive aspect and focus on the little things that might bother them.

Negative self-talk is a manifestation of this type of negative thinking. Some people will usually have a habit of expressing their negative thoughts or feelings in a way that it demotivates them from doing anything productive or good. They are constantly criticizing themselves and lack self-compassion. It's like they have a small voice inside their head that always tries to put them down. This voice can be very convincing and makes the person think that all the self-criticism makes sense. Even if they do one single thing wrong, they think they can't do anything right at all. They will convince themselves that they are not good at something or can't do something right. Instead of trying to do better next time and staying optimistic, they believe that their worst fears will always come true.

Negative self-talk can have negative consequences in your life:

- It makes you convince yourself that you cannot do something. The more you tell yourself this, the more you believe it even if it is not true. '
- You strive for perfection, and nothing less than that will suffice. A single mark makes things completely bad. There is either black or white and no gray area in between.

- Negative self-talk is also linked to depression and can aggravate it. Constantly putting yourself down can make the symptoms of depression more prominent and damaging for your mental health.
- The impact of negative thinking and self-talk is quite immediate in your life:
- It will make you feel worse than you are already feeling.
- It will also be a blockade that will prevent you from getting what you want in life.

Types of negative thinking:

Negative thinking can come in many forms, and all of them are harmful for your wellbeing.

- The all-or-nothing type of thinking makes you feel like a complete failure even if you get a small thing wrong or everything is not perfect to your level.
- The attitude of disqualifying the positive aspects of situations and claiming life to be all bad.

- Negative self-labeling that makes you put yourself down constantly with derogatory terms or sentences.
- A catastrophizing attitude that makes you decide that everything will go wrong even if there is a small incident.
- They think that they can read minds and assume that they know what others are always thinking.
- The habit of using "should" statements, which deem that you should do something or someone else should do something. Such people can be very judgmental if people don't do what this person thinks they should.
- Need approval from others all the time.
- Disregarding the present and thinking of the past or future all the time.
- Many people have a negative, pessimistic attitude where they are never happy with things and always look at the negative aspect. In the glass half full and half empty categories, they fall in the latter.

All these negative types of thinking have an even worse impact when the negative thoughts keep replaying in your head, and you can't seem to control them. This can lead to stress, anxiety, and depression in most people. This is why it is important to recognize and identify those negative thoughts and push it in a more positive direction.

Effect of negative thinking:

- Negative thinking can have a lot of impact on your mind, emotions, behavior, and life in general. It affects you and also the relationship you have with others.
- It does not allow you to lead the worthwhile life that you deserve.
- It causes low self-esteem and lack of self-confidence.
- It decreases the joy and happiness in your life and casts a shadow on it.
- It makes you feel weak instead of strong.
- Negative thoughts are a hindrance to success and pull you down.

- They affect the clarity of your mind and affect your ability to make decisions or think clearly.

It is important to appreciate yourself and your life to be happy. If you allow negative thinking to control you, you lose your chance at a happy life and peace of mind. Negative thinking is at the core of the problem of most mental disorders. It is in your best interest to start focusing on changing this negative train of thought that does not benefit you. It is important to work on being more optimistic and having constructive thoughts instead of destructive thoughts.

Changing your belief system

Some choose to persist in the face of failure while others choose to give up. Some decide to focus all their attention and effort on achieving the goals they set for themselves while others wander. Think of what drives these people and what makes people stay happy even in the face of despair. The answer to this is their belief system. They will react to different circumstances and situations according to their beliefs. Most people have beliefs that are rooted deep in their psyche, and this has developed since their formative years. It is fine if this belief system is positive, but some others have a more negative psyche that needs to be changed. But is it possible to change such a deep-rooted part of someone's mind? The answer is yes.

Let's look at some simple examples. When you sit in a chair, what makes you so sure that it won't break, and you won't fall? Some beliefs are so instilled in us that we don't even notice them, but they are a part of us. When you have a negative mindset, it creates negative beliefs. This is not constructive for you and affects your mental health. This is why it is important to change this kind of belief system. You need to start questioning your belief in all the negative self-talk and negative outcomes that you predict. "What if I won't fail?" "What if people like me?" These kinds of questions need to be asked and thought about rationally instead of beating yourself up about it. Don't create a negative certainty in your mind about everything. Questioning and instilling uncertainty in this negative belief system will be key to changing to a more positive mindset. This will help you grow as an individual and succeed in life. A negative belief system will only hold you back and aggravate mental instability. Thinking in affirmatives is important for a positive attitude.

How to stop negative thoughts and negative self-talk

It is important to create a bridge to positive thinking to defeat negativity. If you want to attract positive things, then you need to put out positive thoughts into the universe as well, this is known as the law of attraction. Negativity only breeds more negativity, and thinking like this will only attract negative events in your life. The important thing to take away from this is that you create your circumstances according to your thoughts and behavior. If you focus on the negative aspects of everything, then you lose sight of the positivity. Your thoughts can act like a magnet to achieve what you want in life. Thinking positively and acting positively will pull positivity towards you as well.

- When you see that negative thoughts come into your mind, don't let them overpower or overwhelm you. Try to stop this stream of negativity before it controls you.
- Use positive affirmations to get rid of negative thinking. Use positive sentences to reaffirm good thoughts. If you work hard for a test, use affirmative sentences to tell yourself that you will pass due to this effort. Don't stress out and think of how you might fail. Getting anxious will be a hindrance in concentrating and writing the test. This applies to any other instance as well. Use these positive affirmations to instill more self-confidence as well. Shift from self-criticizing and focus on empowering yourself. Believing in yourself is crucial to achieve what you want in life.
- Try writing negative thoughts or emotions on a paper and afterwards destroy the paper. If you feel emotions like jealousy or fear, express those in writing, and it will help you release the tension. Then destroy the paper and symbolize the end of the negativity.

- Use reasoning to change negative thinking. Evaluate a thought and rationalize it. Does your rationalization support a positive or negative outcome? Often, there are more chances of good things happening than bad things.

Feeling positive inside will help to bring positivity in our lives. You will attract what you are, so try being positive. If you think of good things, you will start appreciating the good that is already present in your life. Negative thinking does not allow you to take the positives in your life into consideration. All the negative self-talk will cloud your vision and look at your weaknesses instead of harnessing your strengths. It is normal for everyone to have a shortcoming, but there is so much more than you should focus on. Establishing a positive belief system can play an essential role in your life. Try meditation to help in this change. Starting talking in the positive and not negative. Question the negative thoughts and turn them into positives.

Chapter 9

Reducing Stress

Are your work hours too long? Do you feel too tired to spend quality time with your family or friends? Do you feel stuck in a situation? Does it feel like all your plans fail? This is a negative way of thinking that causes stress. Some people learn to identify the problem and deal with it appropriately. Others keep worrying and try to push the problem away instead of resolving it. Stress can have a very negative impact on our mind, body, and life in general. Negative thoughts can increase the stress level and make it more overwhelming. Most people in this day and age will deal with stress in some form or the other. If you ask your grandparents about their youth, you will probably find that their lives were much more stress-free when you compare them to yours. However, this does not take away from the fact that you do have to deal with a lot of stress in your life.

Many reasons can be the cause of your stress, such as:

- Problems in relationships.
- Financial issues.
- Challenging work environment.
- Medical conditions like a chronic illness.
- Prominent changes in your life.
- The death of a loved one.
- Emotional issues like depression or anxiety.
- A traumatic experience.
- Low self-esteem.
- Situations that you are not comfortable with like speaking in public.

All of the above are common causes of stress in the daily lives of most people. However, there are other reasons that we might not have listed but are just as valid.

Symptoms of stress:

Stress can be seen in the form of various symptoms in different people. Some of them include headaches, lack of appetite, binge eating, worrying, lack of concentration, change in sleeping patterns, stomach ulcers, high blood pressure, migraine, etc. These are just a few of the commonly seen symptoms in people suffering from stress. Other than these, it can also aggravate physical issues and affect your immunity. Stress can play a significant role in how you deal with an illness and affect your treatment as well. Nearly everyone is affected by stress in some way or the other. The difference is how they deal with it. Some learn to deal with their stress appropriately, but most get overwhelmed with it, and this affects their life. You need to learn to identify your stressor and see if it is something you can control or not. The key is to try to work with the things that are within your control and change it positively so that you are not faced with more stress. For situations out of your control, acceptance is key.

One of the main things you have to remember is that negative thoughts play a significant role in your mind and any stressful situation. The more negatively you think, the more stressed out you get. This can make your irritable and behave irrationally as well. Your negativity and stress will not just impact you but the people around you and your relationship with them. One of the main aims of cognitive therapy is to change this way of thinking.

Benefits of CBT for stress:

- It will help you understand why some situations trigger stress responses in you.
- You will learn how some of your thinking and behavioral patterns prevent you from feeling good.
- CBT will teach you how to change your way of thinking or behaving so that you can get rid of the stressors in your life and also learn to cope with situations you cannot control.
- You will be more confident about dealing with stressful situations in your present and future.

CBT has been effective for treating severe stress and anxiety for many people. Cognitive and behavioral therapy can help you manage and improve your state of mind and deal with the stress in a better way. Your therapy will depend on how long you have been dealing with stress, your level of confidence, and the intensity of the situations that stress you out. CBT emphasizes that the stress will affect you depending on how you think in certain circumstances. For instance, if your flight gets delayed, you can have two kinds of responses to this. The first will be where you don't think too much about it and listen to some music or catch up on your emails. The other response will be where you think of the delay and your time getting wasted and feel distressed in the situation.

As you can see that your thought pattern will either give you a stressful response to a situation or allow you to stay calm. There are some common cognitive distortions like these that therapists help patients learn to deal with. They help them to identify the common stress triggers and change their thought pattern more positively so that they can stay calm in such situations.

If your situation is not too complex, then six sessions of therapy are most commonly prescribed by the therapist. If you have issues like low self-esteem and anxiety along with the original cause of stress, then the therapist might recommend at least 12 sessions of therapy. Those who have been suffering from stress for a very long time are usually advised to continue for more than 24 sessions and take as long as needed to treat the illness.

CBT works in resolving stress issues by helping people achieve some goals or changes. They can decide to change the way they act like becoming more outgoing instead of waiting for others to approach them. They can try to regulate their feelings and not get overwhelmed with fear or anxiety. CBT also teaches them to solve problems and get rid of thoughts that are self-defeating. It also helps them to deal with issues related to physical illness. Therapists using this process focus on helping the patients to deal with their present and not think of the past. Instead of just their personality, CBT therapists study their thoughts and beliefs to help them.

Compared to many other types of therapy, CBT has been seen to be much more helpful and shows faster results. Many studies have been conducted to compare the results of people being treated with CBT and other types of therapy. The positive results from the research on this therapy have made it a popular approach for most people. If you want to try CBT for treating stress then find a good therapist who will suit your needs.

How to make your life less stressful?

- Start by making time for yourself. You might think that your week is too busy, and you don't have time to relax, but you need to set some time aside for yourself where you have no obligations. Use time management skills to schedule your work and other obligations to stay organized and on track. Take a break in between it all and do something relaxing like going for a walk or a swim. A good rest will help you perform all your tasks better. It will also help you feel better.

- Prioritize and let go of the tasks that are not important. Identify your capacity and take on work accordingly. Taking on more than you can handle will ultimately cause stress. If you have a lot of work piled up, create a list and start with the priorities. Go according to the list so that you know that the main objectives were dealt with. Focus on what is more important.

- Start practicing assertive communication. If you feel like you are being taken advantage of in any relationship, you need to be better at communication. Don't be passive or aggressive but try to find a way to be assertive so that you can put your thoughts and needs forward firmly. People are more responsive to assertive behavior, and it puts forward a clear picture of what you need and feel. Assertive people are respected and respectful. You don't have to be passive to please others and increase your stress levels, but your behavior is important.

- You need to realize that stress also takes a toll on your body and not just your mind. Try to practice some meditation or breathing exercises every day. Deep breathing is a great way to help your body calm down.

- Pay attention to your thoughts. Don't let your thoughts get carried away when you get stressed about something. Stop and analyze whether you are being rational and think of something calmer. If you can't find anything that supports your negative train of thought, then accept that it is unrealistic, and you should stop stressing over it.

- Monitor your moods. CBT exercises for stress management use mood monitoring as a way to recognize negative thought patterns and challenge it. In this exercise, you have to write about a stressful event, how you felt about it, and rate it from 1 to 100 according to how stressful it was for you. Keep this paper and look at it the next day and assess the situation and your reaction. You will be out of that immediate stressful haze to be able to realize what was stressful and what you could do about it instead of worrying about it.

If you find the right therapist or CBT course, you will find it much easier to deal with stressful situations in the future. You will feel more at ease and get better at handling all kinds of situations. This will allow you to stay as stress-free as you can and even avoid most stressful situations in the first place.

Chapter 10

Hypnotherapy

Hypnotherapy is a type of guided hypnosis that is conducted by clinical hypnotherapists to induce a trance-like state. The state induced using this hypnotherapy allows the person to be so focused and concentrated as though they are completely absorbed in some book and cannot listen to anything else. This hypnotic state allows the person to focus inside him or her and find a way to get better. This form of therapy is often used to treat stress or help the patient to break bad habits and many other problems. It is used for a variety of different applications, but it is difficult to assess how effective it is. This hypnotic state is induced to change behavior patterns and help the person find motivation within themselves.

Victorian hypnotists like James Braid practiced the traditional form of hypnotherapy. They used it to directly suggest the patient to remove symptoms like drug abuse or alcohol abuse. Milton H. Erickson developed a different approach to this hypnotism in the 1950s, and this was later known as Ericksonian hypnotherapy. He used informal conversation with therapeutic strategies and complex language patterns in this form of hypnotherapy. However, it was very different from the traditional way so many people questioned its validity as hypnotism.

The early 2000s saw the development of Ericksonian hypnotherapy being combined with solution-focused brief therapy that was goal focused. Then came cognitive-behavioral hypnotherapy or CBH. This uses CBT with clinical hypnosis for greater effectiveness of treatment. This integrated treatment showed a lot of improvement in patients who tried it.

Theodore X. Barber and some of his colleagues published a review of research on this in 1974. They argued that hypnotism was not a special state but a culmination of psychological variables like active imagination and motivation. As more research was done, cognitive as well and behavioral theories were used to explain hypnosis, and this allowed more integration of hypnotherapy with CBT.

Curative hypnotherapy was originated from the work of David Lesser, and thus it is called Lesserian therapy. He understood the possibility of using hypnosis with IMR and questioning to find the causes behind the symptoms of patients. He did not focus on directly trying to push on subconscious information but worked on developing a process to correct wrong information. His work emphasized on the simplicity and logic of the subconscious mind and helped in the creation of the present-day treatment.

As more work and study is done to understand the subconscious, the therapy keeps evolving. The Trance Theory of Mental Illness was put forward by Dr. Peter Marshall. According to this, people who suffer from any neurosis like depression are already living in a state of trance, and it does not have to be induced. Instead, they need to understand the state they are in and the hypnotherapist has to help them come out of it.

Hypnotherapy can be used with CBT to treat many psychological issues like depression, anxiety, substance abuse, phobias, etc. It is used to help people in improving their sleep patterns, communication issues, behavioral problems, and many such related conditions. It is also used for aiding in pain management and resolving medical conditions. Dentists might use hypnotherapy to help patients deal with their fear or treat oral conditions like teeth grinding.

Hypnotherapy is not used as a therapy itself but as an aid with CBT. Finding trained and certified health care professionals for hypnosis is important. The patient should find a hypnotherapist that is qualified but also someone they can resonate with and be comfortable for therapy.

Cognitive Hypnotherapy is a combination of hypnosis with CBT using theories of neuroscience. The natural state of mind that we often find ourselves immersed in like while we read a book or listen to music is the state that is used for therapy in cognitive hypnotherapy. You are not put under someone's control or put into a state where you are helpless. It is just an effective method of helping you to make positive changes. This form of therapy is usually conducted only for a couple of sessions and allows the patient to feel at ease.

Misconceptions about Hypnotherapy:

Hypnosis or hypnotherapy is attached to many misconceptions.

- Some people think that gullible or uneducated people are the only ones who fall prey to hypnosis. They think that being subjected to hypnosis makes a person more gullible. However, this is not true. Hypnosis can only be done when the participant is willing, regardless of how educated or intelligent they are.
- It is a misconception that is commonly thought hypnosis to be a state where the person is asleep or unconscious. It is a state of altered consciousness. It is similar to being focused singularly on an activity and not

paying attention to anything else. The state achieved by meditation is similar to a hypnotized state.

- There is a misconception that hypnosis can be performed against a person's will and can cause you to reveal secrets. This is not true because hypnosis or hypnotherapy does not involve mind control. The person is always in control and will be able to tell if they are being made to do something they are uncomfortable with.
- You don't have to worry about staying stuck in a hypnotic state. People always come out of the hypnotized state at some point. If they don't willingly come back to reality, they might fall asleep and come back to their normal state. No one stays stuck in hypnosis forever.
- People also think that hypnosis can make your mind weaker, but this is not true either. It does not make the person susceptible to the hypnotist's control.
- It is a myth that hypnosis will make you remember everything from your childhood.

- Hypnosis does not necessarily need another hypnotist or hypnotherapist. It can also be self-induced and is called self-hypnosis. It is a skill that can be learned with time and experience.
- There is no single way to enter into a hypnotic state. There are different responses from different people, and each is equally valid.
- Hypnosis is sometimes confused with meditation, which is something that it is not. Meditation is a method of relaxing as the person tries to empty their mind from all thoughts. Hypnosis is induced to achieve something in particular.

Chapter 11

Focusing on the Future

Getting Rid of Toxic Connections

The people in your daily life play a major role in it and your mental health as well. Some people in your life will be uplifting and supportive, and you should keep them around and return the favor. However, there are many more that are toxic connections that need to be severed.

Take a second and think of the people you are always around. Think of that friend you have been friends with for years. Do you notice that she criticizes you far more than she encourages you? Think of the co-worker you hang out with. Have you noticed that he never uses your ideas or praises you in front of others? Your partner can also be someone who constantly puts you down when he should be one of your main sources of support.

Start analyzing your relationships and pick out the weeds that are hindering your growth. This is an important aspect of ensuring your happiness and success. Toxic people will only take from you and have nothing good to contribute to your lie.

If you have a mental illness, you might not have paid attention to this aspect before. But its important to recognize the fact that the people around you also contribute to your mental health and wellbeing. If they are manipulative, aggressive, narcissist or have any such negative tendencies, this is something that will also affect you. You might have known these people your whole life and don't know what to do. It might be a little easier to cut off someone who just entered your life but those who have been around a long time are a little harder to get rid of.

Even though they make you feel bad, you don't know how to sever this connection. However, some people are better at dealing with such toxic people. They recognize the negative impact from this kind of toxic behavior and know how to deal with them. They can either cut them off or learn to not let them affect their lives. People with low self-esteem or lack of confidence will have a hard time doing this. But people with a stronger mental state will be better at managing toxic relationships.

If you need help in managing toxic relationships, here are some tips that will assist you.

Assess situations where you felt rail-roaded by someone. Before shifting the blame on someone else for making you feel bad, reflect on yourself. Do you allow them to talk over you because you fear confrontation or don't have confidence? Think of encounters with these people and try to assess your emotions and actions at the time. What was the reason behind your action and why did you allow the toxic person to make you a victim of their spite? Pay attention to how you react in situations to understand yourself.

Now think about your reactions in situations. Did you react appropriately or overreact or maybe did not react enough? Anyone studying your reactions to another person will be able to make out the dynamic in that relationship. There can be some people in your life who have bullying or narcissistic tendencies. This dynamic is often found in abusive relationships. If you don't react properly to mistreatment and let it slide, it allows the person to think they can continue to behave that way. This is a case of under reaction that causes the situation to escalate. A narcissist will love playing games with an insecure person. An insecure person will fall prey to their games and overreact if they feel like they might lose their relationship with the narcissist. This is because an unhealthy and insecure attachment is in place. This overreaction makes the narcissist feel powerful and reinforces the same cycle.

To deal with these kinds of reactions, it is necessary to learn to manage your emotions. Think over these situations and plan on how you will react the next time. Set some goals to see changes and improve the dynamics in your relationships. Focus on a scenario and think of what you will do when it arises the next time. Think of the words that you should say to make the person realize that you are taking control of yourself and will not allow them to treat you like a pushover. Assertive sentences and body language will help you in this. Standing up for yourself is important if you don't want to allow toxic people to undermine you.

It is also important to trust yourself. An insecure person will be more likely to stay in a toxic relationship. They don't trust themselves to be alone or trust their own judgment. They let the misbehavior of the other person pass by rationalizing that they did not mean it or any other such excuse. Instead of trusting their gut, they choose to give the other person the benefit of doubt. You need to stop making excuses for the misbehavior of others. Think about why you are allowing them to get away with it and try to get yourself out of that pattern. There is no valid rationalization for toxic behavior.

For some reason, all humans tend to hold on and do not like the idea of losing things. This applies to material things as well as the people in their lives. Dealing with any loss is avoided at all cost. However, if a person in your life has no positive contribution to it, is it really a loss? Should you not think of it as a long-term gain when you lose a toxic person? Many people will hold on to toxic relationships because they don't like to think of being alone or think that all their effort would go to waste if they gave up now. They can't think of what would happen after they got out of the toxic relationship because this is what they are familiar with. The fear of the unknown can be a strong factor. This kind of thinking creates an unconscious pattern where you stay stuck in a toxic relationship. Your mind tells you to hold on to something just because you have invested time and effort into it. Instead, you need to start focusing on what you will gain if you let go. The answer will be usually peace of mind and happiness. You will find yourself in a much better place if you get out of the toxic relationship of any kind. This can be your boyfriend, friend, work relationship, etc.

Being optimistic is an advantage. In an unhealthy state of mind, people tend to focus on the negativity and the bad outcomes possible. But in general, most humans are optimistic. They like to think that something good will eventually happen. This is seen easily when you look at people playing slot machines. They keep at it, in the hope that they might get lucky at some point. If you win once, you will keep trying a hundred more times to win one more time.

B.F. Skinner conducted an experiment of intermittent reinforcement. The apparatus included their rats in three cages. There were levers attached to all of the cages to deliver food to them. The first lever always delivered food to the rat so that rat got complacent and knew he would always have food. The second lever did not work, and this rat knew he would not be getting food from it. The third lever worked randomly and sometimes delivered food while sometimes it did not. This meant that the third rat knew that he might get food at some point even if he did not get it a couple of times, so his attention was always focused on the lever. This is intermittent reinforcement, and the same principle works for humans too.

In abusive relationships, it is seen that the abuser is usually mean, but he may also act extremely nice at times. The insecure person will focus on this good behavior and make excuses for bad behavior. They keep telling themselves that things will keep better, and the abuser will act well more often. However, this is not true and not enough reason to stick around. Don't search for scraps of kindness in a relationship that is destructive.

Set boundaries for relationships that cannot be cut off or avoided. This applies when you have family or friends that you will inevitably come in contact with at some point or the other. You know that these people always act negatively towards you and engage in unwarranted criticism but you probably never stood up for yourself. It is important to set boundaries with such people to protect yourself. Call them out if they are rude or inappropriate but not aggressively. Be assertive and display confidence in your manner. Most bullies stand down when they are faced with confidence. If someone crosses a limit at work, report him or her. If someone keeps commenting on how you look, let him or her know that they should not concern themselves about it. If someone makes jokes at your expense, don't go along with it to please others. Take a stand for yourself and let them know that it is not funny. A little sarcasm will do the trick without being directly rude in some cases. For those that you actually can get rid of, do it.

If you decide to stand up to toxic people, you also need to expect retaliation. Such people don't like to lose or feel out of control. If they see you taking control or setting boundaries, they might push harder. They will probably increase their efforts to bring the dynamics back to what they are comfortable with. This can include all sorts of manipulations, bad-mouthing or even physical violence. You need to anticipate and prepare for these types of retaliation. Stand firm and don't let them gain control over you again.

Don't close your eyes to bad behavior. Even if you have been in a toxic relationship for a very long time and are used to it, don't normalize it. Don't make excuses for the person who misbehaves or talks rudely all the time. Bad behavior is not excusable and is not something you should get used to. Don't rationalize someone's harsh words and tell yourself that it doesn't matter. Also, don't let another person ignore you or treat you like your opinion does not matter. This is another type of abusive behavior.

Some liars make excuses when they are caught and try to push the blame on the innocent person. Even physically abusive people make excuses for their behavior by making the victim feel like they pushed them to it. Abuse is not okay whether it is emotional, verbal, or physical. Don't normalize this kind of behavior or allow yourself to get used to it. It is important to call them out and demand respect.

Toxic people make a habit of coming back into your life even when you try to cut them off. It is important to make sure that it is permanent. Don't allow the person to make excuses and try to push their way back into your life. No matter what they say, they will always create problems in your life. Move on from such toxic relationships for good. Treat such separations like a break-up. You know that some relationships have to end when they bring you more pain than happiness or if your partner cheats and lies to you. Let go of these people and don't allow them a chance to come back into your life. You will soon learn that you never needed them and are happier after the breakup.

A lot of toxic people try to act like they are vulnerable and need you around. The truth is that you don't need to be their savior. They are just being manipulative so that you excuse their bad behavior and stick around. They look for your time and attention by acting troubled. When you try to cut toxic people off, they try many different means to keep getting your attention. There can be some toxic friends who always look to you for help. But if you feel like it is overwhelming, then direct them towards someone who can help them. You are not responsible for another person's problems and do not need to burden yourself with them beyond your capability.

The more time that you spend away from toxic people, the more you will feel better. Surround yourself with positive and uplifting people. The energy flow around you will affect your own happiness. Staying around negative people and giving them power over you will only pull you down. If you can't break free of some toxic relationships, then learn to set firm boundaries with them. You need to talk yourself into being more assertive about what is okay with you and what that person needs to change as well. Don't allow people who are toxic to stay in your life and control you. Make time for those who bring you more happiness and work on being happier by yourself as well.

How to let go of the past and build the new you?

Learning to let go is an important step to move forward in your life. Letting go does not always mean that you have to get rid of something, but it means that you will let it be. It is no help to hold on to pain or replay the past in your mind over and over again. Things that happened in the past cannot be changed even if you wish for it. There is no reason to blame yourself and keep thinking of what you should have done either. You have to accept what was and what is and let go. Change is inevitable and to accept it in a healthy manner, it is important to let go. You need to learn to let go of things or people that hurt you as well even if it seems hard. Holding on will prevent you from building a stronger and happier version of yourself. Who you become now will be defined by what you want to be and not by what you were. Your past is a part of your life, but it does not have to define you. Sometimes people get used to the pain and memories and choose to live in that comfortable zone of what they know. It can be intimidating to think of change, but it is necessary. Letting go can seem next to impossible for some people, but it isn't that hard. Here you will learn a few ways to let go and build yourself up.

1. You have to accept that things don't always go as planned and people don't always turn out to be the way we expected them to be. The relationship you have right now might be very different from what you had wanted or expected. Things rarely if ever, turn out to be as we expect them, and it is important to accept this. Acceptance and gratitude will help you improve what you do have right now and make the best of it. You need to trust the process and hope that you will get where you want to be.

2. Try to keep a check on expectations from other people. Expecting too much from another person almost always ends in disappointment. Expectations make you fear

the outcome of things not turning out as you want them to as well. There is no guarantee to how things can turn out or how someone will behave. You need to be more rational about dealing with expectations that are not met. Don't focus on them and learn to let go.

3. Don't limit yourself with negative self-talk. Let go of any inhibitions that don't allow you to move forward and achieve your goals. Keep an open mind and don't limit yourself when you are capable of so much more. The fear of failure can often stop people from even trying, but if you just let go of this fear, you will accomplish much more. Don't allow others to tell you what you can or cannot do either. Use their discouragement as encouragement to prove such people wrong.

4. You need to let go of the notion that you have any control over someone else's actions. You can only control yourself and not another individual who is responsible for themselves. Don't waste your energy in trying to change a toxic person. They can only do this by themselves. Don't try to get

affection and appreciation by doing more for others than you should be doing for yourself. Focus on changing yourself for the better and use your energy on yourself.

5. Stop worrying about what people think of you. Let go of these kinds of worries and think of yourself. Prioritize your feelings and opinions. If you constantly seek approval from others, it can be very pressurizing. Live by your values and don't focus on what others say or think about you.

6. Give yourself leeway for mistakes; you are only human. Let go of trying to be perfect. Use your mistakes to learn lessons. Don't berate yourself over silly things and learn to let go of them. Your mistakes can be funny when you think about them later.

7. Let go of the things that you cannot change. Don't keep thinking of how things could have turned out. Be present in the now. If you want to live your life to the fullest, the present is where it is happening. You have no control over your past, but you can make the right decisions to make your future better.

8. Avoid getting too serious about every single thing. Relax and let some things go at their own flow. Learn to laugh some things off even if they aren't what you wanted or expected. It is all a part of your journey. Taking yourself too seriously will only cause stress and anxiety.

9. Let go of your fears as much as possible. It is human to fear things that can really harm us. But keeping too much fear within you will hold you back from a lot of experiences. Getting out of your comfort zone can be quite crucial at times. Fear will close off the possibilities of your life and block your mind from better thoughts. Facing your fears will make you get over them. It will help you grow and succeed in life.

10. Be expressive about your thoughts and opinions. Use your voice to express yourself. Don't let others overshadow you or ignore your opinions. You matter just as much as anyone else and have the right to express yourself. Communication is also key to finding a good balance in relationships. If

you bottle up your emotions, you allow the frustration to build up inside you. Getting things out makes it easier to deal with them right then. Even if you are angry about something, let the person know right then. If you hold back and keep all the anger inside, it will affect your relationship with that person quite badly. Expression is important for your own mental wellbeing and for better communication with others. Let go of your inhibitions about speaking up.

11. Bereavement or the loss of a loved one is one of the crucial times in your life. Death is inevitable and has to be accepted. Don't try to hold back your feelings at this time. Allow yourself to process your emotions and grieve. There is no shame in crying and grieving. Being hurt or sad at such times is normal. Let go of the feelings and don't try to say strong by holding back. Grieving is a way to honor the dead as well.

12. Let go of grudges. It is important to learn to forgive people. You don't have to necessarily forget what someone did to you.

Remembering will make your more cautious around them. But forgiving will help you move on. The forgiveness is beneficial for you and is not all about the other person. It will definitely make them feel better but don't hold on to grudges to punish them. Holding on to such feelings allows negativity to build up within you. Let go of feelings that hold you back in life and make you live in the past.

It is important to let go of things that hold you back in life. You need to move past what has happened and look towards the future. Holding on to any negative feelings or ideas about yourself will only harm you. These will come in the way of your personal growth and happiness. Stop trying to control everything and accept what is. Letting go of things will help you to learn more about life and yourself.

How to stay positive every day?

Positivity can be very beneficial for your health and happiness. This will only work if you practice it in your actions and thoughts every single day.

Firstly, you need to create the right kind of environment around you. This includes your physical environment and the people you surround yourself with. These factors have a huge effect on your life. Your environment should be conducive to the life you want to live. Surround yourself with people who want to do the same good things that you are trying to do. Find encouraging and supportive friends to hang out with. Join support communities when you are trying to bring a change like combating addictions. Read books or watch videos that are inspiring. Find someone who will hold you accountable for your actions at the end of your day. Make your space positive and filled with things that promote wellbeing. Clean up and keep things neat to make your mind feel the same way as well. A dirty and messy workspace or bedroom is a negative space to be in.

If you want to cultivate good habits in your life, start small. Don't over-do it and put pressure on yourself. Take things one by one and one day at a time. It will help you to incorporate a positive practice into your routine over time. Trying too much at once can be overwhelming and make you want to give up. Go at a pace that you can handle.

Take note of the positive things that happen, or you do every single day. Take a few moments at the end of the day to reflect on it. Your positive thinking will see a surge if you focus on the good. If you focus on the bad, you will build on a negative attitude. Writing or thinking about positive things will make you feel better and keep you in a better mood all day. You will also see that you sleep much better and have less stress levels. A gratitude journal can be helpful in this process.

Start meditating every day. Even if it is just for a couple of minutes in a day, it will make a difference. You have already seen how beneficial mindfulness meditation can be in your life. Meditation helps in improving focus, keeps your mind calm, and improves your mental as well and physical health.

Just starting with two minutes in the morning will have a positive impact on your entire day. It will help you build good habits and see progress in your mental state.

Quick Fix Tips to stay Positive

- Life or circumstances can get hard at any point. In the face of this, it is important to stay positive and not let negative thoughts overwhelm you. I have shared a few effective habits that can help you stay positive in the face of such situations. I hope you find them useful.
- One of the most effective ways is to be optimistic in a negative situation. Even if you stumble upon some hardships, focus on the positive aspects of the situation and what you still have to be grateful for. Also look for a window of opportunity that will help you make things better. This is a much better attitude than complaining about a bad situation. Don't force yourself to ignore the tough situation but take time to process the

fact that there will usually be something that can work to your benefit in any situation.

- Try to cultivate a positive environment and surround yourself with the right kinds of people. Your company matters and should be chosen carefully. Bad company can have a bad influence on you. Find people who support you and contribute to your growth as a person. Take some time to think of the people who are negative influences in your life and distance yourself from them. Also, think of anything you do that has a negative impact on you and stop doing it.

- It is also important to pace yourself. Don't try to get things done in a rush, no matter what they are. This urgency can actually cause stress to build up and affect you. Slow down and take things into perspective as you go about your work. This will help you stay calm and go about things more constructively.

- Don't lose perspective and allow yourself to get stressed over unnecessary things. It is easy to imagine a huge problem arising even when there is a small one. If you find yourself panicking and thinking too much of a problem, try to stop and take a breath. Stop that train of thought and focus on your present as you take deep breaths. Change your focus to gain a wider perspective of the problem and try to find a solution calmly. Also, ask yourself if that same problem will matter in a few years and if you should be stressing over it.

- Don't let self-doubt hold you back from achieving success or happiness. If you want to get things done, you need to take a chance. Don't hold back because you fear you might fail. You might fail, but you might succeed as well so don't doubt yourself. Ask yourself what the worst scenario could be, and you will see that it is something that you will be able to handle. Don't let a vague fear control your actions and stop you from achieving what you want.

- Other than yourself, add positivity to others' lives as well. Giving is an important virtue that has to be harnessed. People will usually treat you how you treat them. Treat them with kindness and compassion, and they will usually do the same for you. Value your relationships with others, and you will see that they will benefit you. Help people if you see they need assistance. It could be in the form of the smallest gestures, but it will matter. You should smile at others more often, and you will see that it is infectious and makes a difference in their day. Be there for people when they need someone to talk to and listen.

- Regular exercise and a good diet are also important. Exercise helps in stimulating happy hormones and also keeps your body healthy. Good food is also important for you to feel good. Being lazy and eating junk food is a negative way to live and does not add quality to your life. Don't try starving yourself to lose weight either. Healthy regular meals will help in stabilizing your mood too.

- Accept healthy criticism. You don't have to fear criticism from other people. Listen and analyze what another person says. If it makes sense and will benefit you, pay attention to the criticism since it is constructive. If someone criticizes you out of spite, be the bigger person and ignore him or her. Also, don't take it to heart or allow it to affect your sense of self-worth. You don't have to immediately reply when someone criticizes you. Stay calm and listen. If it angers you, try taking a few deep breaths. Replying in the heat of the moment will only escalate the problem. Keep an open mind and consider that the criticism might work to your benefit. There is always room for growth for every person. Also, remember that what a person says is not just about you but also reflects on that person himself. Some people project their insecurity on others by using harsh words. Don't take it personally. When you reply to critics, be calm and collected. If it is just a malicious attack, you have to learn to let go for your benefit.

- Learn to let go of steam. If something affects you, don't try to suppress it. Learn how you can react to it better. Share the problem with another person that you trust and ask for their input. Also, work on building a strong sense of self-esteem so that things don't easily affect you or bring you down. Negativity should bounce off you and not get under your skin.

- Always try to start your day positively. This can mean making your bed, drinking some tea, practicing yoga, or doing meditation. Starting your day with meditation or exercise is actually a very positive method. It allows you to start your day with control and in a healthy way. You can also choose to listen to some good music or motivating podcasts to set the mood for the day. You will see that these will make a difference in how the rest of your day goes.

- Be mindful in your thoughts and actions throughout the day. Living in the present makes it harder for negative thoughts or emotions to overtake your thoughts. If you stay in touch with the present and practice positivity, you will see that it is easier to stay happy. If you get bored or start reminiscing, you might start to worry or get stressed again. This will not benefit your mental health. Go through your day at your own pace and be mindful in your actions so that you stay in the present. Try to focus your attention on whatever you are doing or wherever you are at that very moment. Use your senses to connect completely with the present.

All of these regular practices will help you stay positive and maintain a healthy mental state. Try to implement them consciously for a while, and you will soon see that they are a part of your lifestyle. Your negative habits will soon be replaced with these good habits. You need to remember that habits take time to develop so stay persistent in your efforts if you want to see real improvement in your mental health.

Relapse

A possibility of a relapse is always there, but it can be prevented or dealt with when the time comes. The skills learned during therapy will make it easier to control the symptoms of your anxiety or depression if they recur. Don't let go of the skills taught during therapy even if you feel like you are cured.

Maintaining mental health is a constant process. If you take your stability for granted, stressors might cause you to relapse into maladaptive behavior again. However, it is said that those who get treated through CBT have a lower chance of relapsing compared to those who were just treated through medication. If you feel like you can't help yourself, you can always seek guidance from your therapist again.

Chapter 12

Precautions

Cognitive behavioral therapy can be very beneficial for you if you use it in the right way. Here I've enlisted some precautions to keep in mind when you decide to start CBT.

Many techniques are used while treating a person using CBT. It is important to choose the right technique that will help in dealing with your condition in particular. The correct diagnosis and treatment need to be used to see improvement. You need to remember that what works for one person does not necessarily work for another person. Each person has his or her own needs that have to be considered. The right technique needs to be chosen accordingly. Even if CBT does not work for you, you can always try another type of therapy like stress inoculation training. This might help you if CBT does not.

Other than choosing the right kind of therapy, it is also important to choose the right therapist. Just a degree is not enough to show that the person will help in treating your condition. Do some background checks and ask around about good therapists. The best testimonial to their work will be happy patients. Many online sources will help you find out about therapists and their work. Use it to your advantage and find the right fit for you. If you decide not to go to a therapist, you can even try online sources that help in therapy. Make sure you do good research on whatever form of therapy you choose or the therapist as well.

While choosing your treatment and therapist, consider what is feasible for you as well. Some centers or therapists may charge much more than you can or should spend. Choosing an exorbitantly expensive therapist will add to your bills and stress. Use your research to find someone who charges the appropriate rates and has good history with patients. This way you get your money's worth and don't burn a hole in your pocket. If you cannot afford a real therapist, there are Internet therapy courses that will be more cost effective for you. Just find the right one and use it to your benefit.

You also need to remember that things take time. You cannot rush or lengthen the process, as you want. The therapy will last for different times for different people. You need to keep giving your maximum commitment to it to see results. Don't expect major changes in a day or even a week. Give it a couple of months and see how it works for you. If it really does not seem to be helping, then consider another form of therapy or therapist. Don't compare your progress with anyone else at any point. The whole point is to heal your mind, and if you want long-term benefits, then you cannot have short-term effort.

Although CBT is a great form of therapy, keep your expectations reasonable. It works differently for different people and different conditions. There won't be any overnight changes, and you will not become miraculously perfect in a week. Keep at it and watch the little things change and how CBT makes your mental health improve.

If you really want CBT to work for you, keep these precautions in mind.

Conclusion

As you come to the end of this book, I would first like to express my gratitude for choosing this as your source of information. I hope you have found this book informative about Cognitive Behavioral Therapy and that is it is useful to you. All the information has been assembled together after thorough research and put in a way to help you understand it better.

CBT has been recommended all over the world for treatment in mental illnesses due to its effectiveness. Therapists have stopped focusing singularly on drugs for treatment and use CBT for a much more thorough and personal approach towards treatment of mental health. It has been found to help people suffering from depression, personality disorders, behavioral problems and many other issues that are related to mental health.

You can always seek help and try this therapy to help you in healing from depression, anxiety, or any other mental issue you are facing. Giving importance to mental health is just as important as physical health. A healthy body will not be of much use if your mind is in a constant state of negativity. Try cognitive behavioral therapy and see how it helps you to deal with these issues and lead a much better life.

Thank you for your time, and I hope you enjoyed reading this book.

www.ingramcontent.com/pod-product-compliance
Lightning Source LLC
Chambersburg PA
CBHW031113080526
44587CB00011B/959